MADONNA/WHORE COMPLEX

Love without Sex
Sex without Love

MADONNA/WHORE COMPLEX

Love without Sex
Sex without Love

Pat Gaudette

Home & Leisure Publishing, Inc.

Madonna/Whore Complex:
Love without Sex; Sex without Love

Published by
Home & Leisure Publishing, Inc.
P O Box 968
Lecanto, Florida 34460
www.halpi.com

ISBN 978-0-9825617-7-5 (paperback)
ISBN 978-0-9825617-8-2 (e-book)

Library of Congress Control Number: 2011909958

First Edition: July 2011

While the publisher and author have used their best efforts in preparing this
book, they make no representations or warranties with respect to the accuracy
or completeness of the contents of this book. The advice and strategies
contained herein may not be suitable for your situation. This book is not
intended as a substitute for medical advice from a qualified medical
professional. The intent of this book is to provide accurate general
information in regard to the subject matter covered. If medical advice or other
expert help is needed, the services of an appropriate medical professional
should be sought.

The stories that appear in this book are based on the lives of real people who
submitted their stories anonymously through the MadonnaWhore.com
website for inclusion in this book. Names and details have been changed to
protect the confidentiality of these individuals.

Cover image © 2011 Jupiterimages Corporation

Printed in the United States of America

For the woman married to a man who loves her
too much to have sex with her.

Where such men love they have no desire and where they desire they cannot love.—Sigmund Freud, "A Special Type of Object Choice Made by Men," 1910

I love you so much I want to sleep with you, after which I cannot love you anymore, because you are the kind of woman who has sex with men.—Anonymous

Contents

Introduction

I wrote an article about the Madonna/Whore Complex in 1998 when I was the Divorce Support Guide for About.com, an Internet site owned by *The New York Times*, and a position I held for more than nine years. Since then, my original article has been quoted, plagiarized, rewritten, linked to, and even referred to *by* trained professionals. This male sexual dysfunction is not an easy one to identify, is often misunderstood, is not easy to treat, and is embarrassing to talk about.

When I searched the Internet for information about the Madonna/Whore Complex, I became frustrated with the amount of misinformation there is about this male sexual dysfunction. For example:

"Most men want their partners to be virgins in public and whores in bed. Some have two women instead, one respectable wife, a child bearer and one whore."

"Madonna/Whore Syndrome is an out-of-fashion psychological phrase that classically referred to the desire of a man to marry a woman who was publicly pure and privately a vixen."

I receive emails from women who tell me that their husband has stopped wanting to have sex—that "for years" they had a fantastic sex life but lately he just isn't interested so they've decided he must be suffering from the Madonna/ Whore Complex. My usual reply is that he needs to be checked by his doctor to rule out any physical or hormonal reasons as to why his desire has decreased; the Madonna/ Whore marriage wouldn't have years of "fantastic sex" before it tapered off. For anyone dealing with a current lack of desire in their marriage, I recommend two books by Michele Weiner-Davis: *The Sex-Starved Marriage* and *The Sex-Starved Wife*.

After marriage, there's a give and take, a synergy, a tit-for-tat necessary to keep the passion alive and well so that a wife *wants* to be a whore in the bedroom. Some authors believe that the Madonna/Whore Complex is triggered by motherhood such as this excerpt from the book *Practicing Catholic*:

> What makes the conflict universal is the double experience of sex - the necessary means of reproduction and the ecstasy of passionate encounter. Can the spouse and the lover be one? In women, once the progression of generation begins, the maternal can seem to be at odds with the erotic, a tension that can be reduced in male desire to the well-known opposite fantasies of the madonna and the whore.

While some men with the Madonna/Whore Complex have no sexual attraction to their wives after they give birth, childbirth itself does not trigger this lack of passion in all or most men. It is more likely that the roles of mother, wife, and homemaker—and many times career woman—push some women to the brink of exhaustion, changing the sexual dynamics between the couple.

Even though she may want, and have every intention, to be an exciting sex mate, by the time he's ready, she's too tired to get into the mood or be an enthusiastic participant. If their religion forbids any type of birth control, she may be avoiding intimacy in order to avoid having more children—he might be doing the same.

Over the years many men and women have asked me to write more about the complex or to write a book that provides a "cure" for their damaged relationships. The Madonna/Whore Complex isn't an illness so there isn't a cure but having a better understanding of what it is and what it means to relationships between men and women is the start toward making decisions regarding those relationships.

I have written this book because I have been unable to find a book written specifically about this male sexual dysfunction. There are many books that mention the Madonna/Whore Complex and excerpts are included for reference throughout this book.

I am not a psychologist, psychiatrist, trained counselor, or other type of medical professional. This book is written to help assist in understanding the Madonna/Whore Complex, not as a substitute for medical advice or treatment by a qualified medical professional. I was married to a man diagnosed with the Madonna/Whore Complex. That 18-year relationship, and my ongoing research on the issue, gives me intimate knowledge of how this complex affects wives and marriages.

Why have I written this book? Because it's time someone did and it might as well be me.

The Madonna/Whore Complex

He says he loves you but his actions say otherwise. Maybe he's sweet and attentive except when it's time for sexual intimacy; then he isn't interested whatsoever. Maybe he's sweet and attentive except when it's time for sexual intimacy; then he turns into an abusive brute. Maybe he's the most sexually aggressive guy you've ever dated; but why, with all his sweet talk, won't he ask you to marry him? Maybe he's the guy next door with the perfect wife and cute little twins who just got arrested soliciting sex from a police decoy. Maybe he's the shy momma's boy living down the street who celebrates his mother's birthday each year by raping and killing a prostitute.

There are many names for it: Madonna/Whore Complex; Madonna-Whore Syndrome; Virgin/Whore Complex; Prostitute-Versus-Madonna Syndrome; Virgin-Prostitute Syndrome; Pedestal/Gutter Syndrome; Madonna-Whore Dichotomy; Virgin-Madonna-Whore Complex; Madonna vs. Harlot; Obscenity-Purity Complex; Good Girl-Bad Girl Dichotomy. Regardless of the name, it refers to the sexual dysfunction in which some men believe that sex is a dirty act that is only enjoyed by "bad" women—whores. For these men, all women are divided into two very different groups: the whores/prostitutes/harlots, women who are easily seduced and who enjoy the dirty act of sex; and the Madonnas/virgins—as in the Virgin Mary—pure women of virtue who would never enjoy sex and who should not be degraded by the sex act.

Determining the "good" from the "bad" is simple: a woman either has an intact hymen or she doesn't. Hymen = Madonna/virgin; lack of hymen = whore/prostitute. A Madonna would never enjoy sex, a whore would. A man with the Madonna/Whore Complex may have difficulty respecting any woman who would have sex with him. When he looks for a wife, the most important requirement will be that she is a virgin; everything else is secondary.

Few men or women have a neutral opinion of a woman who is openly sexually promiscuous. She's a "slut" or "loose" or acts like a "whore." All of us judge women by their sexual activities, and not in a pleasant way. There is no sexual equality between men and women. Virginity still has a very high value which is why many teen girls consider themselves to be virgins even if they have done every type of sex act possible—except allowing vaginal penetration.

So we're all guilty of judging women as "good" or "bad" based on their virginal appearance, and/or sexual appetites, but the majority of us aren't consumed or obsessed about a female's hymen or lack thereof. But what about those men who are unable to judge a woman by anything else but whether or not she's still a virgin? How do some men become so obsessed with a woman's virginity that they won't marry a non-virgin and they stop having sex with the virgin they marry?

If there's one "ultimate" reference when trying to explain the Madonna/Whore Complex, it has to be Sigmund Freud. Freud believed that from approximately the age of three to six years a boy develops unconscious desires for his mother and a hatred for his father for being a rival for his mother's love. He called this the Oedipus complex and said that a man suffering from the Oedipus complex will look for a mate who is similar to his mother. In Greek mythology, Oedipus unknowingly killed his father and married his mother.

Freud's Oedipus complex begins in late infancy when boys become attached to their first love object, their mother. Freud felt this was a necessary part of the psychological growth of the child but that the attachment must be resolved or outgrown in order to have a normal sexual life as an adult. According to Freud, if the young boy does not progress successfully through the Oedipal phase, there may be unconscious fear of incest when he starts thinking of his wife in the same terms as his mother, along with the fear of castration as punishment for his sexual longings for his mother.

In *Sexuality and the Psychology of Love*, Freud explains why some men are unable to be sexually active with a woman they respect, requiring women who are "ethically inferior" for complete sexual gratification:

> I do not hesitate to lay the responsibility also for this very common condition in the erotic life of civilized men on the two factors operative in absolute psychical impotence, namely, the very strong incestuous fixation of childhood and the frustration by reality suffered during adolescence. It has an ugly sound and a paradoxical as well, but nevertheless it must be said that whoever is to be really free and happy in love must have

overcome his deference for women and come to terms with the idea of incest with mother or sister. Anyone who in the face of this test subjects himself to serious self-examination will indubitably find that at the bottom of his heart he too regards the sexual act as something degrading, which soils and contaminates not only the body. And he will only be able to look for the origin of this attitude, which he will certainly not willingly acknowledge, in that period of his youth in which his sexual passions were already strongly developed but in which gratification of them with an object outside the family was almost as completely prohibited as with an incestuous one.

A man who was never able to bond to a cold and distant mother might choose women like his mother in order to fulfill earlier unmet intimacy needs. A man raised by an overly attentive mother might not have outgrown his early fixation and seek a mate who resembles her in personality as well as appearance. In both instances the man's needs and motivations would be at a subconscious level. A man given up for adoption, who never was able to experience the early bonding of infant to mother, may look for a mother substitute to fulfill that need. Regardless of what repressed or unresolved issues form his beliefs, when his wife becomes a mother substitute, he will lose sexual desire for her.

Not all of his peers were in agreement with Freud's theories regarding the reasons for dysfunctional sexuality. However, his theories have been quoted the most when trying to explain the causes of the Madonna/Whore Complex (or whatever other name this particular male sexual dysfunction is given).

The following is from the Abstract of "Sigmund Freud and His Impact on Our Understanding of Male Sexual Dysfunction" by Ume Hartmann:

While some of Freud's theories are obsolete today, many parts of his work appear to be astonishingly modern, even in the light of current neurobiological research and recent models of sexual dysfunction. Above all, Freud was an extremely gifted observer of human behavior who shows us that in many cases, sexual dysfunctions are no isolated phenomena, but have their roots in biographically based intrapsychic or interpersonal conflicts.

And this is the Abstract of "Freud's psychology and its organic foundation: sexuality and mind-body interactionism," by B. Silverstein:

Although Freud's neurological education had a great impact on his thinking, a review of Freud's early writings reveals that: (1) Freud adhered to a mind-body interactionist position that was not in accord with the mechanistic neurology of his medical school education; (2) Freud saw psychical processes as intentional, not completely determined by mechanical brain processes—but interactive with them; (3) Freud made functional and psychological interpretations freely without accepting a need to "neurologize" his psychological insights by providing specific neuroanatomical or neurophysiological correlates for such interpretations; and (4) Freud sought the organic base for his evolving psychology in sexual physiology, not neuroanatomy or neurophysiology.

The Oedipus complex is scrutinized in David E. Stannard's *Shrinking History: On Freud and the Failure of Psychohistory*. This excerpt discusses the results of a study by Stanley M. Friedman:

... We must recall that the theory of the Oedipus complex is multifaceted: it postulates that the complex derives from the child's jealousy of the parental performance of the sex act and, further, that there are specific adult personality patterns that arise from the repressed Oedipus complex. Neither of these matters was confirmed or even tested by Friedman, nor have they been

successfully tested by anyone else. Friedman's findings can be seen, then, as possibly important, but very limited. They show that in a particular cultural setting support was found for the hypothesis that, though not openly admitted, boys of all ages show a greater degree of hostility for their fathers than for their mothers and girls from the same age distribution show a greater degree of hostility for their mothers than for their fathers.

Some regression therapists believe that problems occur shortly after conception and throughout the time in the womb, culminating with the actual birth experience. Alice Rose, Ph.D., a clinical psychologist, and author of *Bonds of Fire: Rekindling Sexual Rapture*, says if the gestation or the actual birth are full of trauma or extremely painful physically and/or emotionally, the buried memories can return when a man gets into a close and loving relationship with a woman, causing him to push away from her.

Psychoanalyst Donald W. Winnicott felt that problems originated earlier in childhood, prior to the oedipal phase according to this excerpt from *Freud and Beyond: A History of Modern Psychoanalytic Thought* by Stephen A. Mitchell and Margaret J. Black:

...Winnicott argued that fundamental disorders in selfhood originate prior to the oedipal phase (to which Freud had traced neurosis), even prior to later infancy (to which Melanie Klein had traced depressive disorders). Winnicott's most profound and most productive insight was the connection he began to draw between false self disorders in adult patients and the subject variations he observed in mother-infant interactions from the very beginning of life. What seemed most telling was not gross abusiveness or severe deprivation, but something in the quality of the mother's responsiveness to the baby, her "management" of the baby's needs. It was not just feeding that was crucial, but

love, not need gratification, but the mother's rewsponsiveness to the "personal" features of the infant's experience.

Attachment theorists, beginning with English researcher John Bowlby in the late 1930s, focus on a child's emotional attachment to his or her mother or primary caregiver during early childhood. According to *Theories of Attachment: An Introduction to Bowlby, Ainsworth, Gerber, Brazelton, Kennell, and Klaus* by Carol Garhart Mooney:

> *Most contemporary theorists assume that what does and doesn't happen during the earliest stages of life affect development for a lifetime in powerful ways. Unmet needs in infancy continue to haunt us until they are eventually reconciled.*

In *Becoming Attached: First Relationships and How They Shape Our Capacity to Love,* Robert Karen writes:

> *Further research would eventually establish that separations, even long separations, do not in themselves cause a child to become a psychopathic personality. It's the depriving separation that's so calamitous, where the child never has a chance to develop a true attachment; where there's no alternative mother figure to take up where the first mother left off and perhaps to keep her memory alive; or where there are, early on, a series of short-term mother figures and thus repeated losses, all of which cause a bitterness and mistrust to develop and the shutting down in the child of his natural tendency to reach out for love and connection.*

As a result of childhood attachment experiences, according to attachment theorists, people develop into one of three adult attachment types: secure, anxious, or avoidant. The following description of the avoidant person is excerpted from *Attachment in Adulthood, Structure, Dynamics, and Change* by Mario Mikulincer, PhD, and Phillip R. Shaver, PhD:

> *People with an avoidant attachment style cannot risk allowing emotion to flow freely and be acknowledged*

consciously. Avoidant defenses are largely designed to inhibit emotional states that are incongruent with the goal of keeping the attachment system deactivated (Main & Weston, 1982). Defensive inhibition is directed mainly at fear, anxiety, anger, sadness, shame, guilt, and distress, because these emotions are triggered by threats and can cause unwanted activation of the attachment system. In addition, anger implies emotional involvement in a relationship, and such involvement may undermine an avoidant person's commitment to self-reliance (Cassidy, 1994), Moreover, fear, anxiety, sadness, shame, and guilt can be interpreted as signs of weakness or vulnerability, which contract an avoidant person's sense of strength and independence. Avoidant individuals may even feel uncomfortable with joy and happiness, because they promote interpersonal closeness and may be interpreted by a relationship partner as indications of investment in the relationship (Cassidy, 1994).

Avoidant individuals also attempt to block emotional reactions to the potential or actual unavailability of attachment figures (rejection, separation, loss), because such reactions imply neediness and dependence. Like secure people, avoidant ones attempt to down-regulate threat-related emotions. But whereas secure people's regulatory efforts usually promote communication, compromise, and relationship maintenance or repair, avoidant people's efforts are aimed at minimizing closeness and interdependence, regardless of the deleterious effects on a relationship.

Religious teachings can also play a major role in a young man's upbringing, influencing his sexual behavior. In his book *Sexy Origins and Intimate Things*, author Charles Panati writes:

Until quite recently, for instance, the Catholic church maintained that the only reason for a husband and wife to have sex was to conceive a child. In the last 1960s, when American women were burning their bras in the women's liberation revolution, Pope Paul VI addressed an audience of obstetricians and gynecologists in Rome, telling them how their profession must view each and every woman:

"Woman is a vision of virginal purity which restores the highest moral and emotional sentiments of the human heart... She is the creature most docile, singing, praying, yearning, weeping, she seems to converge naturally towards and unique and supreme figure, immaculate and sorrowful, which a privileged Woman, blessed among all, was destined to become, the Virgin Mother of Christ, Mary."

In stating that every living woman 'seems to converge naturally towards' the immaculate Virgin Mary, the pontiff reinforced the centuries-old impossible role of woman as virgin and wife/mother - the madonna-whore syndrome.

Even though we are considered to live in an age of sexual freedom, old attitudes about female sexuality still abound and pop up to cause problems in couples' relationships. This is an excerpt from a paper titled "Clinical Assessment in the Treatment of Sexual Dysfunctions" by W. Charles Lobitz and Gretchen K. Lobitz, which is included in the *Handbook of Sex Therapy*:

A second category of inappropriate cognitions are destructive attitudes that inhibit sexual arousal. The most common of these is the "good girl-bad girl" dichotomy. Despite a liberalization of our culture's attitudes toward female sexuality, many of our patients maintain the belief that there are two mutually exclusive kinds of women: those who are sexually responsive and sexually active and those who are good wives, mothers, and citizens. Whether this belief is held consciously or unconsciously, it results in the woman subtly being reinforced by her partner and herself for being responsible, conscientious, and unsexy. If a woman's self-image includes this dichotomy, she will always be in conflict about her sexual arousal. Furthermore, if her partner also holds this belief, not only will he unwittingly discourage her sexual responsiveness but also he may be in conflict about his arousal in response to her.

This belief on the part of the man is frequently most manifest by his arousal to erotic literature, magazines, movies, and fantasies, but not to his partner. In this example, one clue to the existence of sexually destructive attitudes is the patient's sexual developmental history. For example, a recent patient was taught by his parents that "nice girls" are not interested in sex. Although he might have had an opportunity to prove this untrue with girls in his peer group, in early adolescence his family moved to a more upper-middle-class community where he did not have a peer group that immediately accepted him. Desiring social acceptance and cognizant of his parents teachings, he restrained himself from any behavior that might be termed sexually aggressive with all girls whom he dated. This included anything more than hand-holding. Prior to meeting and marrying his wife, his sexual behavior consisted exclusively of masturbation to erotic literature and fantasies and, occasionally, intercourse with prostitutes.

A sentence that got my attention, also in the *Handbook of Sex Therapy,* appears midway through a paper titled "Impotence as a Practical Problem," written by John Reckless and Nancy Geiger: *"The fourth design centers around castration anxiety; oedipal feelings and incestuous fantasies fuse when a man marries a 'good' partner 'just like mother.' "*

In *Falling in Love: Why We Choose the Lovers We Choose,* author Ayala Malach Pines writes this regarding Freud's Oedipus complex:

When boys and girls do not pass through the Oedipal stage successfully, they remain fixated at this stage and cannot detach themselves from their infantile love object. When they grow up, such men remain in love with their mothers and are incapable of loving fully other women. Typically, they get married and declare that they 'adore' their wives, who invariably are 'wonderful mothers.' But, for some 'inexplicable reason,' they are not attracted to their wives sexually. They are, however, attracted sexually to all other women, but they never love any of these women. Their love is reserved for the mother who is their wife. This type of split has been termed the whore/Madonna complex.

In her book *Leaving Him Behind: Cutting the Cord and Breaking Free After the Marriage Ends* author Sandra S. Kahn writes:

> While the emotional baggage carried by women who came of age in the forties, fifties, and early sixties has to do with the old "sex is dirty" myth, men's baggage often contains the old and terribly destructive madonna/whore complex. This is the idea that (1) good women are mothers, and (2) bad women love sex, but (3) these qualities are never found in the same woman. In this myth, motherhood is sullied by sexual responsiveness, and sexual responsiveness is eradicated by motherhood. Many men still believe in this duality and trap their wives into this orientation. It's an easy step from idealizing "the mother of my children" within the marriage to viewing a woman as a tramp once she is free to see other men.

In their book *Clinical Manual of Sexual Disorders*, Richard Balon and Robert Taylor Segraves list several variations on what they call "partner avoidance" including one they call "The Don Juan casualty":

> A man has consistently used seduction of women to entertain himself. Quite proud of his accomplishments, he views sex as sport and may pride himself on the large number of female friends he can occasionally can to get together sexually. He marries a woman he considers terrific but has little desire for her. This is often seen in marriages between a young woman and a much older man who regards his wife as a "prize." In some psychiatric circles, a Don Juan is referred to as a phallic narcissist or as suffering from a Madonna-whore complex (Freud 1905/1953). This character type has been known cross-culturally in literature and music for centuries.

Theorist Robert Wright, in his book *The Moral Animal*, traces the sexual double standard back to males' need to know that their children really are their own. Wright thinks that Victorian attitudes to sexuality are essentially in tune with evolutionary reality. What he calls the "Madonna/whore dichotomy" has, he thinks, been imprinted on the male mind by evolution with men seeking women who aren't promiscuous so that they (the men) can be certain they're raising their biological children and not some other lover's.

While some people believe the Victorian-age sexual double standard is over, Wright isn't so sure:

> There is a tendency these days to reject and scoff at these aspects of Victorian morality. Rejecting them is fine, but to scoff at them is to overestimate our own moral advancement. The fact is that many men still speak openly about "sluts" and their proper use: great for recreation, but not for marriage. And even men (such as well-educated liberal ones) who wouldn't dream of talking like that may in fact act like that. Women sometimes complain about seemingly enlightened men who lavish respectful attention on them but then, after sex on the first or second date, never call again, as if early sex had turned the woman into a pariah. Similarly, while the double standard has waned in this century, it is still strong enough for women to complain about. Understanding the Victorian sexual climate can take us some distance toward understanding today's sexual climate.

In her book *Men Who Can't Be Faithful: How to Pick Up the Pieces When He's Breaking Your Heart,* author Carol Botwin writes:

> For many men, womanizing is the result of looking at women as either pure beings or whores. The Pedestal/Gutter Syndrome they suffer from accompanies many other psychological motivations for infidelity. For men with this mind-set, women are divided into two classes—you are either good (on a pedestal) or bad (in the gutter). If you are thought of as the "good" woman, you are admired, but not thought of as sexual. Bad women,

whom these men look down upon either consciously or subconsciously, are the erotically alluring ones. An example of this is one man who came into couples therapy with his wife as the result of an affair. He described the other woman in his life as cheap, vulgar, kind of dumb. When asked why, if he felt this way, he found her so attractive, he replied, "She's sexy." For some men, because of religious teachings or the way they were brought up by their parents, any woman, no matter how elegant, can be thought of as bad simply because she is having sex outside of marriage—only bad girls do that!

In his book *The Clintons Meet Freud: A Psychohistory of Bill, Hillary and Chelsea*, psychiatrist Paul Loweringer writes about Bill Clinton's relationships with his wife, his mother, and his mistresses. According to Lowinger:

This is the classic psychoanalytic dilemma of the Madonna (not the pop star) and the Whore for a man who is impotent with his wife but potent with a mistress. His wife represents the mother, a tabooed sexual object, while the bad woman is permitted sexually so he has another kind of Oedipal problem. Bill's mother image is split by the power of the Oedipal prohibition into a good mother-wife who becomes forbidden as a sexual object and a witch or bad mother who is allowed because she is degraded by the sexuality denied to the wife.

But there was an earlier Oedipal obstacle to be surmounted. Bill's first solution to his Oedipal dilemma was to escape from the taboo against Mother Virginia's steamy Southern sexuality into Hillary's cooler Yankee persona. In an Oedipal confession, Virginia says she wanted him to choose an Arkansas beauty queen like her rather then Hillary, the hippie intellectual Chicagoan with coke bottle glasses. But after a few years of marriage his libido returns to the Arkansas beauty queens, groupies and Gennifer. Why? The Madonna/Whore dilemma was back with a new cast and now Hillary was the taboo Oedipal good mother. Hillary had blended with Virginia and had gone from Whore to Madonna in the unconscious of Bill Clinton.

In his book *If Men Could Talk: Unlocking the Secret Language of Men,* author Alon Gratch writes:

> *What's the opposite of a thing called mother? You might raise an eyebrow. Freud thought it was a thing called whore. Freud observed what he called the Madonna/Whore complex, which, the sexual revolution notwithstanding, is still a problem plaguing many men. In this situation the man treats his wife or girlfriend with so much respect that he is reluctant to sexually objectify her. He will engage in certain sexual fantasies or acts only with other, less respected women. This sexual split is an important way in which men manage their aggression, or more accurately, manage to hide their aggression - from others as well as themselves.*

In *Secret Lives of Great Authors,* Robert Schnakenberg writes this about the private life of Franz Kafka:

> *He regularly patronized various Prague brothels and enjoyed a seemingly endless succession of one-night stands with barmaids, waitresses, and shopgirls—if you can call it enjoyment. Kafka was revolted by sex and suffered from a pronounced Madonna/whore complex. He considered every woman he encountered either a virgin or a slut and wanted nothing to do with them once he was physically gratified. The idea of 'normal' married life disgusted him. 'Coitus is the punishment for the happiness of being together,' he wrote in his diary.*

In Victorian times anatomical virginity—an intact hymen—was the concern of a girl's parents as well as her future husband, as explained in this excerpt from *The Body Project: An Intimate History of American Girls* by Joan Jacobs Brumberg:

> *A century ago, the hymen was a meaningful membrane with enormous social and emotional value. Although middle-class Victorian prudery made discussion of sex and genitalia highly offensive, the hymen was nevertheless on people's minds. The typical Victorian counselor told young female readers that they*

each had a "jewel" or "treasure" worthy of preservation until it was appropriately (and legally) sacrificed at marriage on a sweet "hymeneal altar." Because an intact hymen was a prerequisite to a good middle-class marriage, many mothers and fathers had a vested interest in its preservation. Future husbands were also concerned about it, because a bride who came without a tight hymen was regarded as damaged goods. In this context, a girl's hymen was in effect "jointly owned" by her family and her bridegroom as much as by the girl itself.

Regardless of what the initial cause of his Madonna/Whore Complex was, the man's beliefs are ingrained in him; they are as much a part of him as his hair color and a lot more difficult to change—if he even wants to change them.

While there are varying degrees of Madonna/Whore Complex—some which have quite severe consequences for women and are discussed in a later chapter—typically a man suffering from the complex chooses a sexually inexperienced woman for his wife and places her on a very high and lonely pedestal in order to worship her goodness and virtue. He may have been very sexually aggressive before marriage but that's because he didn't have a deep love for her and he was testing to see if she would be easy to seduce or would remain a "good girl" despite his pressure and promises. The "good" girl is the one he brings home to Mother.

When he finds the woman who survives his critical eye and marries her, his sexual passion for her vanishes. Sex with her becomes a duty he will perform as infrequently as possible and without any of the fantasies he might try with other women he may be sexually active with. When his wife gives birth to a child, *their* sexual intimacy will become virtually non-existent. If he remains sexually active—as some men with this dysfunction do while married—it will be outside the marriage. He may indeed have a "Madonna" at home and a "whore" in his second bedroom—wherever that may be.

A man with this complex may have a very strong attachment to his mother even after marriage; his mother may remain the most important woman in his life—much to the dismay of his wife who may have considered his devotion to his mother a sign that he was good husband material. On the other hand, a man with the complex might despise his mother. His issue with women stems from a positive or a negative interaction with his mother, or a mother figure, early in his life.

Because of low self-esteem issues, he may believe that his wife could be easily seduced into having sex with someone else. Even if his wife denies having interest in other men, he may become obsessed in tracking her every move to be sure that she isn't seeing a lover during those times she's out of his sight.

My former husband demanded that I call him on the hour every hour and check in with him. Rather than face his wrath and accusations, I watched the clock and was prompt to call. He wanted details about my location and who I was with. After I answered his questions, he would tell me he loved me and then I had to say "I love you" back to him, loudly, so that anyone nearby could not help but overhear.

A young woman who marries a Madonna/Whore man may not have even the slightest clue that there is something very wrong within their relationship. She may be thrilled to have found a man who places her on such a lofty pedestal, who worships her, who is so concerned for her well-being. Her joy will fade over time as she discovers that, as much as he worships her, he also loves her too much to soil her with such a dirty act as sex.

A sexually inexperienced woman may think it is her very inexperience that is responsible for her husband's lack of desire for her, that the problem is hers to fix. Over time, she will question her attractiveness, wondering if there is a way to make herself more sexually appealing to him. Her attempts at sexual seduction by actions or appearance may backfire with him accusing her of acting or looking like a whore. His rejection will be a terrible blow to her increasingly fragile self-esteem. It is a particularly cruel blow when she sees the interest her husband shows in other women.

For even the most inexperienced woman, sex and love are a package deal. Marriage, for women who are taught "good girls don't," is supposed to be when "good girls do." Marrying a man with the Madonna/Whore Complex usually means that "good girls won't" *after* marriage either. Sex, for women married to such men, is infrequent and passionless. When she has a child, there is even more sexual distance. Once he sees his wife in the role of mother, the link between his wife and his mother is complete and he has even more reason not to "defile" her with the "dirty act" of sex.

Perhaps Freud or other researchers were correct as to early developmental issues that set the stage for the Madonna/Whore Complex. Maybe his mother constantly told him sex was nasty, or she caught him masturbating and screamed that only bad boys did that. Maybe as a very young child he was in the room while his parents were having sex and what he saw and heard translated in his infant brain into something bad. Or his religion taught him that sex should be for procreation not recreation, that any form of birth control was murder, or that most sexual expression was evil.

There are situations in which a man with the Madonna/Whore complex marries a woman with beliefs the same as his. For example, couples with strong Catholic upbringings steeped in the belief that birth control is wrong and sex for anything other than procreation is a sin, may have large families or fairly sexless marriages. Eventually, if his wife refuses to have sex, his needs may drive him to seek it elsewhere while his wife turns a blind eye to his infidelity because, as her mother always warned her: "Men will be men."

Neither the husband nor the wife in a Madonna/Whore marriage may understand why they are so unhappy in their relationship. He loves her but he doesn't want to be sexually intimate with her. She loves him but she is increasingly bitter because he won't give her the sexual intimacy she desperately craves. Infidelity may be a cornerstone of their marriage, as he seeks sex elsewhere to satisfy his needs and she takes lovers to validate her self-worth.

In some cultures it is not uncommon for husbands and wives to lose interest in sex with each other, their marriages becoming fairly asexual, once the children are born. The behavior may be as a result of societal influence, but it has mother-Madonna roots. This lack of interest in sex does not extend outside of the marriage, and in some societies it is expected that the husband will have lovers. It is less expected that the wife will also have a lover. In such cultures, divorce is less of a threat than in cultures where men and women are seen as equals with equal sexual needs.

Male sexual dysfunctions are less discussed than female sexual dysfunctions but occasionally a famous personality's bedroom behavior becomes front page news. The plethora of media attention regarding Tiger Wood's multiple mistresses, his treatment for sex addiction, and divorce from the mother of his two children is one example. His sexual activities might indicate a Madonna/Whore influence.

Elvis Presley might be the most famous celebrity who may have suffered from the Madonna/Whore Complex. His devotion to his mother was absolute and her influence was evident throughout his life but probably not any more than when he was searching for the ideal girl to make his wife. Despite his involvement with many beautiful women, including some of Hollywood's top starlets, he reached far outside the Hollywood dating pond to find the woman good enough to bring home to mother. During his tour of duty in Germany, he met 14-year-old Priscilla Beaulieu, the virginal girl he would try to make over in his mother's image.

For a man afflicted with the Madonna/Whore Complex, the only type of woman good enough to be his wife is a woman like his mother, or the image he believes his mother to be—unblemished and sexually pure. Elvis was involved with many women but only Priscilla qualified for placement on the pedestal reserved for his wife. It gets lonely on that pedestal, as every "Madonna" wife soon learns. Regardless of how much emotional love there might be between the two of them, if he is unwilling to express that love through sexual intimacy it may eventually destroy the marriage.

Only Priscilla Beaulieu Presley knows what happened or didn't happen in her marital bedroom. She alludes to problems within her marriage in her book *Elvis and Me* when she says Elvis' lack of desire for her after the birth of their child was causing her "to doubt my own sexuality as a woman." She writes this about the relationship Elvis had with his mother:

> *"When Elvis's mother was alive they had been unusually close. Elvis even told her about his amatory adventures, and many nights when she was ill, he would sleep with her. All the girls he took out seriously had to fulfill Gladys's requirements of the ideal woman. And as with me, Elvis then put the girl on a pedestal, 'saving her' until the time was sacred and right. He had his wild times, his flings, but any girl he came home to he had to respect."*

The woman married to a man who suffers from the Madonna/Whore Complex knows exactly what Priscilla Presley is describing, the type of loneliness she faced, the embarrassment she would have felt, her growing hostility that he was getting his sexual needs taken care of elsewhere by women more sexually appealing to him than she was.

Did Elvis Presley, that mega super sexy hunk of burning love, have a problem with sexual intimacy with his wife? From the little amount Priscilla Presley shares about their intimate times it appears he did. Add in his strong attachment to his mother and his steady stream of sexual partners—who were physical opposites of his wife and his mother—and it is very probable that he suffered from the Madonna/Whore Complex or what author Carol Botwin calls the Pedestal/ Gutter Syndrome:

Elvis Presley suffered from the Pedestal/Gutter Syndrome. He valued the fact that his wife, Priscilla, was an unsullied virgin when he met her. Soon after he married her he lost sexual interest in her and started sleeping with other women whom he didn't respect as much as Priscilla, but who were able to excite his sexual interest.

Warning Signs

So how can a woman avoid dating and/or marrying a man with the Madonna/Whore Complex? Are there any warning signs that would alert her to this type of man? The answer is an unhelpful "yes" and "no."

A man with the Madonna/Whore Complex isn't particularly easy to spot and many with the complex may be so charming that any woman would consider herself lucky to be in a relationship with such a man. Men can be charming without suffering from this complex so that's not a warning sign, per se.

He may be the perfect son, always considerate of his mother's feelings and they may have a very close relationship. Many girls are told by their mothers to watch how a man treats *his* mother and choose a man who treats her well as that is a sign he will also treat his wife well. That's true if the man and his mother have a mutually respectful relationship; it's trouble for his future wife if their relationship has Madonna/Whore roots. Closeness with his mother isn't always a tip-off; some men with the complex despise their mothers.

They've been dating long enough that she wants their relationship to turn into the total commitment of marriage but he remains elusive. He *says* he's in love with her, so why not commit? Many men won't make the marriage commitment if they don't have to. If he suffers from the Madonna/Whore Complex and she has prior sexual experience, she has a slim to none chance at the gold ring or the pedestal this man reserves for his wife.

He may love her *sexually* but he doesn't love her *like he would his mother*. Settle down and start a family? Not hardly! He's completely happy playing the field and going home to mother at the end of the night. When he does marry, his mother substitute—his Madonna wife—will be waiting at home for him.

He may have a playboy reputation because of the number and type of women he dates. "Stud" and "horn dog" may be terms his peers use in conversations about his sexually active lifestyle. Even though his male friends may be envious of his success with women they don't realize that dating is serious business to him as he sorts the women he dates into two types— virgins for love, everyone else for sex.

When this man begins dating a woman, he will test her to see whether she is "good" or "easy" since he believes most women are whores. If she is sexually experienced when they begin dating, she will immediately move into the category of whore. If she's a virgin but has sex with him too quickly, by his personal measure, she will move from the category of potential wife into the category of whore. His reasoning is, if it was easy to get her to have sex with him, she would just as easily have sex with someone else, and that warrants her placement in the "for sex" group. He'll still go out with the "bad" girls but he already knows they're not going home to meet his mother.

The reluctant virgin who passes this man's purity tests may be pursued, wooed, won, married, loved, protected, and treasured. She will also be emotionally and verbally abused as she struggles with his refusal to be physically intimate with her. Because of her lack of sexual experience, it may take longer for her sexual intimacy needs to surface but when they do, she will have to deal with overwhelming frustration, confusion, and even the type of embarrassment alluded to in Priscilla Presley's book.

Not every Madonna/Whore marriage is fraught with problems. Some women are taught from an early age that sex should be for procreation only, never just for recreation. Because she isn't comfortable with recreational sex, this particular Madonna wife is relieved her husband leaves her alone and gets his sexual needs met elsewhere as long as she isn't publicly embarrassed and the security of her marital home isn't threatened.

Some women may be asexual, or trying to come to terms with bisexuality or homosexuality, or simply may not enjoy physical intimacy. Any of these could be the reason they were still virgins and why they didn't give up their virginity without a mighty struggle—if they gave it up at all—and why they might not have a problem being in a Madonna/Whore marriage.

"Good girls don't" has been taught to generations of young men and women. While she has been cautioned to keep her "legs crossed," he has been told "wear a raincoat," and "don't get her pregnant" — or "you break it, you bought it." On the wedding night that was all supposed to change with the new wife ready and eager to switch from "good girl" to "wanton wife" — except in the Madonna/Whore marriage where the wife is expected to keep herself pure from "dirty sexual urges."

Youthful hormones and young love usually meant marriage often took place before relationships had matured and before couples knew each other well enough to make the lifetime commitment dictated by their marriage vows. Once reality took hold and their differences surfaced, it was usually too late for anything other than "sticking it out" at least until family responsibilities were taken care of, which, for most couples, may have meant divorce at midlife.

The man with the Madonna/Whore Complex both enjoys and is disgusted by the sex act. He cannot love a woman who was sexually active before they met; "true love" and virginity are a package deal for him. There is no forgiveness for a one time "mistake" that results in a girl losing her most precious commodity, her hymen, even if she was deeply in love at the time. It's a "one strike you're out" mentality that allows him to easily determine who could be and who won't be his future wife.

If he does get emotionally involved with someone who he thinks is a virgin and then discovers that she has been sexually active prior to their relationship, he may become obsessed with her sexual history, wanting to know everything about her previous lover(s) and the most intimate details of their sexual encounters. He may think of little else except her sexual experiences with a former lover even if the relationship has been over for several years. Because he is emotionally invested in the relationship with her, he may be unable to just walk away but he is also unable to forgive her for not holding onto her virginity until she met him. *"Why couldn't you have been strong enough to wait?"* he might ask her time and time again as he continually relives her sexual history in excruciatingly intimate detail.

Here's how two men, who may be dealing with Madonna/Whore issues, have expressed their feelings about their wives' prior sexual history. The first man is several years younger than his wife:

I've always been very intimidated by my wife's past. It started from me reading intimate details of her diaries about a year into our relationship. The person I thought I knew and who she told me she was didn't measure up to what I read in her diaries. This lead to issues.

She was older than me and her friends made fun of her because I was "just an 18 year-old kid." So I've always felt I needed to measure up and surpass everyone she knew. After all these years, I still feel the same way.

Now, somehow, I can't get the mental images of my wife with her ex's out of my head!!! I know what they look like, I know the details of her past, this is not good! It's not that what she did is wrong, it's not, it's that I can't stop playing the movie in my head!

It's not about "getting over it." It's about "Stop thinking about it!!!" I will never come to terms with it. It's just better left untouched. But it's hard when I'm reminded about it randomly by random events.

I've read that there are men married for 20,30,40 years who obsess about these thoughts. I've heard of individuals who find out their significant other was a stripper or escort before they were married. They still love their wife, but they can't shake the thoughts of "what if this" or "what if that?"

I know what we have is unique and shared between us... blah blah blah. Well, it's the only thing I've ever known so as far as I'm concerned, every relationship is like this. I know what chocolate tastes like... but nothing else, so all food must taste like chocolate. And it's a double-edged sword, because either my wife has shared the same love with others she's shared with me (which makes it the same $hit, just a different pile), or it's different, which makes me want to experience and understand that! I feel like I've totally missed out on some of the most important experiences life has to offer. Either that, or there's something missing in my relationship? Something that's making me feel like there's a big void in my heart.

As I was driving yesterday, I practically burst into tears when putting the pieces together that it felt like the entire base I've got under me is crumbling. I find strength in my family and my mother. I always did. My mom is as solid as a rock. When my parents divorced and my dad became an alcoholic, my mom was the perfect shining star in my life... That is, until I met my wife.

It's not that my wife became my mother, it's when my wife and I first started dating, my mother obviously opposed it. That's when "the rock" rapidly pushed the transition from her to my own independence.

This next man has been in a long-term marriage and just recently feelings about his wife's past have surfaced to cause him anxiety:

After more than 20 years of a blissful, perfect relationship with a girl that dotes on me, one morning, quite out of the blue, I woke up with a horrible feeling:

1. How could my wife have stayed faithful for so long? She's a good looking girl and had no shortage of admirers.

2. Other men have hit on her, guys in nightclubs, colleagues etc. and she's always brushed them off, but I started blaming her for it (in my head) and feeling hurt.

3. I started remembering times she's had to go away on business and imagining horrible scenarios, like it was a scam to go and see another man.

4. I started obsessing about "what if's", imagining that the most mundane situation could have escalated to the point of a split up, then feeling hurt as if she had actually considered it.

5. I started wondering if she had ever had second thoughts about me and if so, I reasoned that our relationship wasn't as strong and great as I had always thought it to be.

6. Then it turned really horrible. I started asking myself how she could be the morally correct person I thought her to be if she had slept with someone before me.

7. Then I decided her love for me wasn't as strong and true as I had thought because she had a physical relationship before me.

8. This turned into a belief that her previous boyfriend would always be special and on her mind—"a girl never forgets her first"—even if she left him because he was abusive.

I've answered all these questions, found peace and put them back in the box they came from, but the hurt still lingers. I just don't know why it still hurts. Maybe it's just habit now. I know I don't like the thought that she ever liked anyone but me and I don't like it that she had a life before me.

I hate the jealousy and possessiveness in that statement, it's not my way, and it's never bothered me before. I was always content with a real world perfect relationship - to me, real world perfection includes human frailties, genuine mistakes etc., but now it seems my head needs fairytale perfection and can't accept that it's not a reasonable aspiration.

I feel hurt, like her past was something done to hurt me, or it makes what we have less special. When I think of it in adult terms, I see that the past was just ordinary juvenile relationships that mean nothing and can't hurt me, but at other times the thought of my wife with someone else crushes me and I react like a child—I want to say "it's not fair" and I feel full of self pity.

The Virginity Issue

How important is a female's virginity? For the man with the Madonna/Whore Complex it is his only measure of whether a woman is good enough to love. How does a man get this belief ingrained into his value system? Freud and others point toward an event during early infancy or childhood; others point to religious teachings. The "good" girl/"bad" girl dichotomy is constantly played out in literature, and in the media.

It's rare that the "bad" girl ends up with the "hero" as happened to Julia Robert's character in "Pretty Woman." Most love stories follow a familiar theme with the "good" girl getting the "hero" by the end of the story. As important as an intact hymen has been throughout history, and as much as we're conditioned by what we read and watch, it's a wonder more men don't judge the value of a woman by whether or not this small piece of skin is still in place when they begin a relationship with her.

In March 2011, Egypt's military arrested female protestors during a demonstration in Cairo and performed "virginity tests" on them; the women were also strip searched in full view of male soldiers including some who were taking pictures of the women. When questioned, the authorities said they needed to protect themselves from charges of rape. They then made the results of the "tests" public saying that none of the women were virgins.

Historically, it has been important for a woman to have an intact hymen at the time of marriage as proof of her virginity. In some societies, a bride who does not have an intact hymen is returned to her parents, subjected to public ridicule, physically punished, or even put to death. In modern Japan and Italy, plastic surgeons are kept busy by reconstructing the hymens of many engaged women to create "neovirginity" for those who wish to conceal their sexual histories from their future husbands.

Virginity testing is common in India where "impure" brides are forced to name their lovers; the lovers are then forced to pay large sums of money to the bride's family. In Turkey, a new bride's virginity is extremely important, and many women undergo virginity tests against their will. In South Africa, virginity tests are seen as a way to safeguard against AIDS; proof of virginity sometimes backfires because of a myth that AIDS can be cured by having sexual intercourse with a virgin.

In *Mary: A Flesh-and-Blood Biography of the Virgin Mother*, author Lesley Hazleton writes:

> We still think of being virgin as being innocent. Innocent, that is, of sex. But this surely begs the question of why we should be innocent of sex. To be innocent is to be free from moral wrong, to be guiltless, to have done no evil. Do we then think of sex as morally wrong, guilty, and evil? Whatever modern reason says, our language betrays us. This may be the twenty-first century, but some part of us still subscribes to the antiquated dualisms

*of virgin and whore, good girl and bad girl, innocent and slut—
terms that exist in abundance for girls and women, but hardly at
all for boys and men, among whom sexual experience is at least
tolerated and usually appreciated.*

*The idea of virginity as a precious commodity that can be
lost —not through carelessness, but more in the sense of a 'lost
soul,' doomed and damned—is often rationalized by the idea of
wholeness. From this point of view, an intact hymen is the visible
evidence of a state of perfection. Once it is gone, the female
body is no longer whole, but becomes used or damaged goods.*

The following excerpt from *Masters and Johnson on Sex
and Human Loving* by Robert Kolodny and Virginia E. Johnson
was so outrageous—in my opinion—that I wanted to research
it further:

*According to the Code of Hammurabi, a set of laws
established in Babylonia about 4,000 years ago, a man who
raped a betrothed virgin was to be put to death. If a man raped
a married woman, however, both the rapist and his victim were
regarded as guilty and were executed by drowning. A similar
distinction with a slightly different twist was found in biblical
injunctions about rape (Deuteronomy 22: 22-28): a married
woman who was raped was seen as a willing accomplice, so
she and her rapist were killed; a virgin was considered guilty
only if she was raped in the city, since it was assumed that her
screams would have lead to her rescue. In contrast, a virgin
who was raped in a field outside the city walls was spared, since
no one could hear her screaming. If she was betrothed to
someone, her rapist was stoned to death—if not, he had to marry
her (whether or not she liked this arrangement didn't seem to
matter).*

The following are the Old Testament passages from the
King James Version of the *Bible*:

*Exodus 22.16-17: And if a man entice a maid that is not
betrothed, and lie with her, he shall surely endow her to be his*

wife. If her father utterly refuse to give her unto him, he shall pay money according to the dowry of virgins.

Deuteronomy 22.13-21: If any man take a wife, and go in unto her, and hate her, [14]and give occasions of speech against her, and bring up an evil name upon her, and say, I took this woman, and when I came to her, I found her not a maid: [15]then shall the father of the damsel, and her mother, take and bring forth the tokens of the damsels virginity unto the elders of the city in the gate: a[16aaa]nd the damsels father shall say unto the elders, I gave my daughter unto this man to wife, and he hateth her; [17]and, lo, he hath given occasions of speech against her, saying, I found not thy daughter a maid; and yet these are the tokens of my daughters virginity. And they shall spread the cloth before the elders of the city. [18]And the elders of that city shall take that man and chastise him; [19]and they shall amerce him in an hundred shekels of silver, and give them unto the father of the damsel, because he hath brought up an evil name upon a virgin of Israel: and she shall be his wife; he may not put her away all his days. [20]But if this thing be true, and the tokens of virginity be not found for the damsel: t[21]hen they shall bring out the damsel to the door of her fathers house, and the men of her city shall stone her with stones that she die: because she hath wrought folly in Israel, to play the whore in her fathers house: so shalt thou put evil away from among you.

Deuteronomy 22.23-27: If a damsel that is a virgin be betrothed unto an husband, and a man find her in the city, and lie with her; then ye shall bring them both out unto the gate of that city, and ye shall stone them with stones that they die; the damsel, because she cried not, being in the city; and the man, because he hath humbled his neighbours wife; so thou shall put away evil from among you. But if a man find a betrothed damsel in the field, and the man force her, and lie with her: then the man only that lay with her shall die. But unto the damsel thou shalt do nothing; there is in the damsel no sin worthy of death: for as when a man riseth against his neighbour, and slayeth him, even so is this matter: for he found her in the field, and the betrothed damsel cried, and there was none to save her.

Deuteronomy 22.28-30: If a man find a damsel that is a virgin, which is not betrothed, and lay hold on her, and lie with her, and they be found; then the man that lay with her shall give unto the damsels father fifty shekels of silver, and she shall be his wife; because he hath humbled her, he may not put her away all his days. A man shall not take his fathers wife, nor discover his fathers skirt.

In his book *Sexy Origins and Intimate Things: The Rites and Rituals of Straights, Gays, Bis, Drags, Trans, Virgins, and Others,* author Charles Panati writes about religion's role in helping to shape the way men and women view sex:

The view of women as temptresses, sinners, necessary evils, and second-class citizens is ancient in most patriarchal societies. In the Western world, it reached a frightening peak and became misogyny in the early centuries of Christianity. With Jesus Christ's birth mother - also a lifelong virgin - held up as the idealization of womanhood and the model to which every Christian woman should aspire, a woman was supposed to bear children but never sully herself with sexual thoughts or pleasures. This impossible 'virgin-mother' image, which contradicts the biology of nature, has generated repercussions that still resonate.

In his book *Can Love Last? The Fate of Romance over Time,* author Stephen A. Mitchell writes:

Many men of our time struggle with a modified version of the Madonna/whore complex that was such a powerful motif for the Victorian gentlemen of Freud's day. Now it is often presented in terms not of the saintly Madonna versus the degenerate whore but of proper, more respectable women versus women who give themselves to sexual abandon, or of the familiar and dependable woman versus the anonymous and unknown woman who is ready for adventure. Many women of our time similarly struggle with a split between love for men they see as "nice" or "good," dependable and responsible, and desire for men they see as exciting, reckless, and at least a little dangerous.

In *A Virgin Conceived: Mary and Classical Representations of Virginity,* author Mary F. Foskett writes:

Although Greco-Roman sources detail the punishments incurred by women caught in adultery, relatively little mention is made of non-priestly female who relinquished their virginity prior to marriage. Perhaps the Roman custom of marrying elite females at an early age rendered such circumstances improbable. Of such virgins, Peter Brown writes:

"Too labile a creature to be allowed the periods of sexual freedom granted to young men, and tolerated even in husbands, her family must guard her carefully... The girl's loss of virginity was, simply, a bad omen for her future conduct. A girl who had already enjoyed furtive love affairs might do the same when married. She was not a 'well brought up' girl."

Loss of honor was the price paid by a virgin who allowed herself to be seduced.

In their book *Sex Work: Writings by Woman in the Sex Industry,* authors Frederique Delacoste and Priscilla Alexander discuss the differences in which the sexual experiences of men and women are viewed:

Whereas chastity as impurity refers to identity, unchastity as defilement refers to experience. Female virginity is commonly considered the opposite of defilement: the virgin is unspoiled and the defiled girl (or woman) is "spoiled." Non-virginity refers specifically to sexual experience; defilement refers to physical as well as sexual pollution or violation. Boys and men are not stigmatized by (heterosexual) non-virginity or defilement. In fact, the lost innocence which devalues girls is apt to raise the status of boys. Sex and violence dishonor women and honor men. Women are stigmatized with The Scarlet Letter; men are rewarded with The Red Badge of Courage. Her shame is his honor.

Most traditionally, a girl is supposed to remain a virgin until she marries at which time her husband "takes her." If she should engage in sexual relations before marriage, then she becomes unchaste and, in some cultures, uneligible for a marriage of standing. Whether the sex was voluntary or imposed is irrelevant to the social damage incurred through the loss of virginity. If the sex was imposed then, on the one hand, the girl can at least claim passivity; on the other hand, imposition implies the double damage of sex and abuse. In either case, girls are stigmatized as whores once they have been exposed to sex, by force or by choice.

In her book *Maiden USA: Girl Icons Come of Age (Mediated Youth)* by Kathleen Sweeney discusses teen sex and the disparity between boys and girls' responsibilities regarding the sex act:

The male "need" for genital "release" as taught links to the unconscious, to sleep, to a "he can't help himself" equation that in heterosexual relationships names girls as the gatekeepers of sexual relations. Boys are encoded as unable to control themselves; girls are taught that not only can they control themselves, but they must; it's part of their job description. If they don't control themselves and their boyfriends, they will end up pregnant and it will be their own responsibility to resolve.

Post-Lewinsky and the blurring of semantics about what constitutes the sex act, "Good Girls" will masturbate their boyfriends or provide oral sex to "help them" channel their desire with the assumption that they remain intact Virgins in the process. Teenage girls do not have a codified outlet for their desire without risk of being ostracized as weird, dirty, or Sluts. The issue of a girl's reputation remains much more strictly codified. While guys are sometimes jocularly labeled "man-whores" for sleeping around, it is mostly in a joking code among girls as a warning not to expect much in terms of commitment from them. Promiscuous Guys are not judged, ostracized, or whispered about, they're just the roosters in the henhouse, strutting around.

The lengths to which some parents will go to protect a daughter's virginity is described in *Yes Means Yes: Visions of Female Sexual Power and a World Without Rape* by Jaclyn Friedman and Jessica Valenti:

> Sexualizing girls isn't jut about enforcing beauty standards - it's also about reinforcing traditional gender roles and the purity norm. Take purity balls, for example. At these promlike events, fathers escort their young daughters to a party where at some point - between the dancing, the food, and the entertainment - the girls will recite a pledge vowing to be chaste until marriage, and will name their fathers as the "keepers" of their virginity until a husband takes their place. The fathers will also pledge to "cover" their daughters and protect their purity:

> "I, [daughter's name]'s father, choose before God to cover my daughter as her authority and protection in the area of purity. I will be pure in my own life as a man, husband, and father. I will be a man of integrity and accountability as I lead, guide, and pray over my daughter and as the high priest in my home. This covering will be used by God to influence generations to come."

In her book *He's a Stud, She's a Slut, and 49 Other Double Standards Every Woman Should Know* author Jessica Valenti writes about Purity Balls:

> ...The most recent incarnation of the sexual double standard being played out in a seriously creepy way is through Purity Balls. These prom like events basically have fathers take their daughters to a big fancy dance where they promise their daddy their virginity. Likewise, the father promises to be the "keeper" of his daughter's virginity until he decides to give it to her future husband. Where are the Purity Balls for the men, you ask? Oh, they're there, but they're about controlling women too! Called Integrity Balls, these events focus on men not having sex because they'd be defiling someone else's "future wife"! Not because men need to be pure or be virgins - but because they need to make sure women are virgins.

You would think that in today's more "enlightened" age virginity wouldn't hold the same importance as in the past, that women have value with or without an intact hymen. Unfortunately, you'd be wrong according to *The Purity Myth: How America's Obsession with Virginity Is Hurting Young Women* by Jessica Valenti:

> Women are pushing themselves and punishing themselves every day in order to fit into the narrow model of morality that virginity has afforded them. Some of us get unnecessary plastic surgery—down to our vaginas, which can be tightened, clipped, and "revirginized"—in order to seem younger. Others simply buy into old-school gender norms of ownership, dependence and perpetual girlhood.
>
> ...If we're to truly understand the purity myth, we have to recognize that this modernized virgin/whore dichotomy is not only leading young women to damage themselves by internalizing the double standard, but also contributing to a social and political climate that is increasingly antagonistic to women and our rights.

The Making of a Madonna Wife

I had just turned 20 and was extremely naïve about sex when I met the man I would marry. I truly was clueless about the actual sex act and even reading stories in my mother's stash of trashy women's magazines didn't help explain exactly what "doing it" involved. The story line in the various "confession" magazines was pretty basic: the "bad" girl had sex before marriage and the "good" girl waited. For her promiscuity, the bad girl suffered various terrible fates including losing the guy she loved. The good girl, on the other hand, married the man of her dreams and went on to wedded bliss which started with a honeymoon of glorious sexual awakening.

What I read about the dangers of premarital sex was in agreement with my mother's view of sex before marriage (and possibility my mother's view of sex in general): giving up my virginity before marriage was one of the worst sins I could commit—the direct road to Hell—and no "decent" man would want to marry me if I wasn't a virgin on my wedding night. As far as marital sex, she said it was a duty a wife endured after marriage but she implied it was not a particularly pleasurable one.

My peer group was fairly conservative and we talked about many things but never about sex. Sure, we talked about boys but it never occurred to me that my high school friends might be having sex during their make-out sessions with their boyfriends. I regarded sex in terms of black and white: only sluts did it before marriage—that fit well with my mother's words and the stories in the magazines hidden in the back of her closet.

I was slow to mature and while my girlfriends were dealing with their nesting urges and the surging hormones of their boyfriends, I was still wishing someone would ask me out on a date. It was not difficult for me to remain virginal; I rarely dated and the few guys who did ask me out weren't sexually aggressive.

I was just a couple weeks past my twentieth birthday when I met the man I would marry three years later. It was a chance meeting at a drive-in restaurant in a part of town that I didn't normally frequent. My girlfriend was a curb hop at the restaurant to help pay her college expenses. I'd met Linda while in college and we remained casual friends after I quit and went to work full-time in an office. Her love life was chaotic, she fell in "love" frequently, but no relationship lasted very long. She was what we used to call "loose."

I had no love life but that didn't stop Linda from asking me for advice about the problems she was having in her various relationships. Considering that my experience consisted of one very short and chaste relationship just after high school that was the result of a blind date, all I could really do was listen and provide sympathy which is pretty much all Linda wanted anyway.

On this particular Saturday night, as we sat in my red sports car and munched on burgers and fries, a man pulled into the space next to ours. Linda looked over and recognized him as one of the regulars at the drive-in. They said "hi" and then she introduced me to him. He had a cup of coffee and left.

A couple days later he called my house and asked if I'd like to go out on a date. Linda had given him my phone number no doubt in an effort to make up for going after (and getting) a guy I had a crush on at the college. We arranged to go out to dinner and a movie the next evening.

He was smiling as I opened the door to invite him in to meet my parents but his smile froze and he was quick to hustle me out of the house and into his car, slam the door, and demand to know what the joke was. He was furious and I was confused. He wanted to know what kind of game "my sister" was playing and wouldn't believe me when I said I didn't have a sister, that there was no joke. I had to show him my driver's license to prove that I was actually the same person he had met a few evenings before.

Sitting in my red sports car, a flowing scarf around my head and wearing dark sunglasses, I presented a much different image. He expected a date with sports car girl, not the shy, modestly dressed girl sitting in his car. He handed my driver's license back, put the car in gear, and drove in silence to a drive-in theater.

I don't know what movie was playing. He sat in stony silence and I was huddled against the passenger's door. At intermission he bought me a box of popcorn and a coke. We left before the second feature ended and he drove me straight home, not bothering to shut off the car engine or get out and open my car door. He was gone before I got to my door.

The next day, as I was driving home from work, I saw him sitting at a traffic light; he was on duty. I pulled up next to his police motorcycle and gunned my car's engine. He looked over, the light turned green, and I roared off. He followed and pulled me over. He asked me to meet him for coffee that evening and later, as we talked over coffee, I remember thinking "I could marry this man."

Our second date was the beginning of an on-and-off courtship that spanned three and a half years. Within a month, we were "going steady" and by the end of the year he bought me an engagement ring. The ring came before we had sexual intercourse but not before he had convinced himself that I was a virgin and not until I made it extremely clear that I would not be giving up my virginity until I was in my bridal bed.

It didn't take too many dates for Tony to get around to my sexual experience and he didn't believe me when I said that I was a virgin. A 20-year-old virgin? Impossible! Of course that meant he had to prove that I was lying and each date we went on became a grope fest. I'd never dated someone who was so focused on touching all my private parts. The few men I'd dated before Tony had been reserved and occasionally as shy as I was. I'd never had to fight to keep my clothes on.

Each date we had was pretty much the same. He had an image to keep up with his guy friends and I didn't fit the image they expected of his girlfriends. So, we avoided going places that he might run into anyone he knew. I later figured out that also kept us from running into his other girlfriends.

We may or may not grab a burger somewhere. Maybe we'd go to a drive-in movie—never an indoor one. If we went to a drive-in movie it turned into a make-out session. Or we'd park somewhere remote and make out.

My shyness at having him expose my miniscule breasts during our make-out sessions was minor compared to having him try to put his hand under my panties. Many nights ended with him angry and me determined that he was not going to touch me "there" *ever!*

He also wanted me to touch *him* "there" and after much reluctance, I did. Once I'd touched him, he kept pushing until I learned how to give him a "blow job." Once I had been trained in oral sex, every make-out session ended with me performing oral sex on him.

Finally, when he did touch me "there," he drew back in amazement. "You really *are* a virgin," he said in awe. Whatever he felt in "there" confirmed what I had been telling him all along.

The quest to "pop my cherry," as he crudely put it, then began in earnest and nine months after we began dating, we "did it" for the first time on the couch in his parents' living room, while they slept in a back bedroom. It was not glorious and he didn't hold me afterward and tell me how much he loved me; he told me to go clean myself up. I went into the bathroom, ran some water, and waited for five minutes so he'd think I knew what I was doing although I didn't.

He hadn't used a condom, I wasn't on birth control, and I had no clue about preventing pregnancy. Apparently God looks out for foolish girls because in all the time we dated, I never got pregnant. Once we'd had sexual intercourse there was no reason not to continue; my virginity was gone and stopping sex wasn't going to bring it back.

Our relationship changed after that night. He stopped pressing for sex and "making out" wasn't his top priority as it had been previously when we went out. He also began double-dating me, taking me out for a couple hours then going home "for an early night's rest."

After several weeks of his indifference about dating and sex, I borrowed the neighbor's car and staked out his house. It didn't take more than one stake-out to discover that his other girlfriend was a buxom red-headed barmaid with two small children.

During the years that we dated, we broke up several times due to his cheating. Even though he dated a number of women while we were "engaged," he was terrified that I would start dating and that some other guy would defile "his" property. Despite catching him cheating on multiple occasions, I always forgave him thinking that his cheating was probably justified because I was such a poor lover.

The sad truth was, regardless of how bad a boyfriend he was, I wasn't going anywhere. Once we had sex, I felt he owned me; he felt the same.

Despite opposition from our families, particularly both mothers, and my own second thoughts, we eloped and were married by a justice of the peace in another town. I was excited to be married and had fantasies of a romantic and intimate wedding night but that didn't happen, nor did Tony make any attempts at seduction in the following nights. When we got home, I was speechless when he told me very matter-of-factly that we would have sex once every other Saturday night (and not *that* Saturday night; we'd wait for two weeks), in order to prevent sex from becoming boring and causing problems in our marriage.

The proposed twice a month encounters usually didn't happen. When Saturday night arrived, Tony would groom himself meticulously and dress in his best clothes for a night out with one of his friends. I knew better than to challenge him, and because married women didn't "go out" on "date night," I spent the night home alone. He would return home well after midnight—sometimes just before dawn— seemingly too tired to do anything other than sleep. If I asked where he had been he would say he and his buddy visited a few bars, stopped to talk over coffee, and the time got away from them. I knew the guy he went out with had a string of girlfriends even though his wife was a blonde bombshell. When I got an STD after one of Tony's "we were just talking" nights out with his buddy, the pretense that we'd have sex ended.

It was very clear that Tony didn't want to make love to me and when I finally got the courage to ask why, he said I wasn't sexy enough, that I should wear sexy lingerie to turn him on. He knew I had very low self-esteem about my body and probably thought this would put an end to the issue but I was determined to do as he asked despite how uncomfortable I felt in my own skin.

The following week I went shopping at the local *Fredericks of Hollywood* and bought some sheer baby doll lingerie. The next afternoon, after swallowing my embarrassment and putting on the sexy lingerie he wanted me to wear, I waited for him to get home. He walked in the door and stopped.

There was a second of dead silence before he scowled and said *"You disgust me! Go put some clothes on!"* Even now, decades later, I still feel a blush of discomfort remembering his words, the tone of his voice, and the look on his face.

I wasn't ready to give up on making myself attractive to him. If lingerie didn't work maybe a new hairstyle would: "You look like a whore." I usually wore business suits to work; maybe I needed to wear more feminine clothes: "You dress like a whore."

Along with his disparaging remarks about my appearance, Tony began questioning if I was having an affair. Other women might have taken a lover in order to repair their shattered ego but I was not morally equipped to betray my marriage vows regardless of how badly my husband's actions damaged my self-esteem or if he had no respect for the marital vows.

Even if I wouldn't have been morally against adultery, I suspected that Tony was capable of physical violence if he caught me cheating. Later I realized his accusations were probably due to his cheating; if he was cheating, I had to be. It didn't matter that he didn't want me; he didn't want anyone else to want me or me to want anyone else. I was his personal property—just as I had been when we were dating.

His efforts to control my time out of his sight were extreme. If I was at work, he would call at random times during the day and demand my full attention. Once he was sure I was paying attention to him, he would make small talk and then tell me he loved me and wait for me to say it back to him. If I didn't say it loudly enough so that everyone in the office could overhear, he would tell me to repeat my words until there was no doubt that everyone had heard. I was embarrassed to play such a sick game but not complying brought angry repercussions once I got home. He never physically abused me but the emotional and verbal abuse took its toll.

On days that I worked out of the office he demanded that I call him "each hour at the top of the hour" — not one minute early, not one minute late — regardless of where I was or what I was doing. Each call ended only after I proclaimed loudly that I loved him. It didn't take long for me to figure out that this was his way of guaranteeing that I wasn't with a lover or, if I was, my lover had heard me tell my husband I loved him.

Sex happened one or twice a year and only when I became so frustrated and desperate that I begged him to make love to me. What I got for my begging was the opportunity to perform fellatio on him while he lay motionless on our bed. There was no reciprocal touching, no foreplay. I was fully clothed; he was naked. While he was putting his clothes on, after I brought him to climax, he would ask with a smirk "Do you feel better *now*?" I wanted to shout "No! I don't! I need sex!" but I knew it was pointless.

I got married believing that any marriage was a lifetime situation, good or bad. I think much of that came from my parents staying together when there was very little love and certainly not much "like" in their marriage. It took me years of agonizing about the rights and wrongs of divorce before I decided anything was better than remaining in such a cold relationship as my marriage had been. Tony demanded to know who "he" was when I told him I was divorcing him.

He was sure I had a lover waiting for me, that I'd never be able to leave on my own.

I certainly had issues of my own that kept me dating Tony and that kept me in a dysfunctional marriage but as I "grew up" and resolved some of my earlier issues, I knew that if I didn't get away from him I would die emotionally. I couldn't live any longer in a loveless relationship, knowing that I'd never feel the passion other women felt, never feel the love that other women shared with their husbands.

In the early years of our marriage I thought I was to blame for Tony's cheating, his refusal to make love to me, the lack of warmth between us. He couldn't tell me the truth because he didn't know the truth in those early days. When a psychiatrist said he had the Madonna/Whore Complex a few years into our marriage, I had hopes that therapy would improve our relationship, but it didn't. There was no change in his attitude or how he treated me during the years he spent in therapy and I got the feeling that the sessions, both individual and group, were focused on giving him confidence that he was okay as he was.

Is He or Isn't He?

You may be wondering if the lack of sexual interest your husband displays toward you is due to the Madonna/Whore Complex. A married man whose sex drive decreases after years of activity does not suffer from the Madonna/Whore Complex. This is not a condition that comes on later in life, it is a condition that starts early in his sexual development. There are many other reasons for a man's sex drive to decrease including disease, injury, hormonal changes, stress, and extramarital affairs.

The man suffering from the Madonna/Whore Complex can have some strange ideas regarding women and sex. I was appalled when Tony told me that a woman could be "forgiven" for being raped only if she was killed by her rapist. His warped reasoning was that any woman who had sex with a man, consensual or not, had "asked for it" in some way by her actions, her dress, or being in a situation that would allow sex to take place. The rapist was not wrong, she was.

He and his mother may have an unusually strong attachment to each other, a relationship so strong that the wife feels like a third wheel in her marriage. Tony's mother despised me, continually sabotaging my efforts to fit into their family before and after our marriage. Shortly after we were married she told him that the worst day of her life was the day he married me.

If he talks about sex at all, he probably talks about it negatively, as something that "nice" people don't talk about, and may use childish terms for the breasts and genitalia. Tony referred to my breasts once during our marriage; he called them "moo moos."

He may be overly antagonistic about any type of pairings that he considers to be "unnatural" such as same sex or interracial couples. For him, there is only one "right way" as far as who should be having sex and how they should be doing it (missionary style); anything other than vaginal penetration he doesn't consider sex.

Does his religion teach that sex for anything other than procreation is evil, that good women do not enjoy the sex act, and that his natural urges are unclean? What about the family dynamic? Do his parents have an openly affectionate relationship or are they rigidly inflexible particularly about anything sexual in nature?

In her book *Men Who Can't Be Faithful: How to Pick Up the Pieces When He's Breaking Your Heart,* author Carol Botwin writes:

> *When a man is single, he may take a woman out for a long time but never try to sleep with her. But he has an active sex life on the side with women he thinks are sluts, or he may even patronize prostitutes. Or he may be able to be highly sexual with a woman as long as he isn't committed to her, but the minute he cares for her or moves in with her, for example, or becomes engaged to her or marries her, sex disintegrates because she suddenly becomes the good, pure woman in his eyes and is therefore asexual.*

The actual diagnosis of Madonna/Whore Complex should be made by a trained professional who may also be able to help treat the man diagnosed with the complex. Therapy won't necessarily mean a change in the type of relationship a man has with his wife or other women. Not all therapists try to change a person's thinking; some therapists focus on allowing a man to become more comfortable with his existing beliefs and behaviors.

The Wives and Girlfriends

As I was compiling the first draft of this book, I set up a website at MadonnaWhore.com which included a contact form for anyone who would be willing to submit their story for inclusion in this book. I received submissions from both men and women.

Cassie, the Girlfriend

Cassie wrote that she had recently ended a four-year relationship with a man she said fits the profile of a man with the Madonna/Whore Complex. She says they had *"wonderful and amazing sex"* until they moved in together and then the sex stopped and he kept making excuses as to why he was never in the mood. She says that his very close relationship with his mother *"has always been inappropriate and I'm sure there are emotional improprieties there"* and that he needs to *"cut the apron strings."* She feels *"emotionally scarred"* and has very low self-esteem as a result of the experience.

"Yes, I must say that it is easy (in a way) to stay with a Madonna Whore Man because of the true benefits of being the Madonna. You are on a pedestal and he respects you and holds you dear. After a while, though, you realize that he doesn't associate sex with love at

all. While he's attracted sexually to other women and claims to be deeply in love with you, he simply won't make love to you. My boyfriend kept saying that he wasn't sexually attracted to me, but wanted to marry me. It was so contradictory—it just didn't make any sense, especially when we had amazing sex during the first year.

The person that ended the relationship was me. I realized what was going on and broke up with him. I don't THINK he cheated on me, but who knows? If he wasn't getting it at home, he had to get it somewhere. My sexual history is pretty normal. I've never had this problem before with any boyfriends. Sex was a regular part of our relationship."

Ruth, the Wife

Ruth wrote after reading the article on my website. She said that her husband didn't initiate sex after they got married and completely stopped after they'd been married just a couple of months. She thinks much of his behavior matches that of a man with the Madonna/Whore Complex.

"He likes to hug me, kiss me a lot but not have sex. We loved each other dearly and had great sex before the marriage. Now we have been married 2+ years and I just found out he has been cheating on me for more than a year. He wants to get divorced after I found out his affair. But he still keeps telling me that he still loves me in a brother and sister way and he cannot have sex with me because he has no desire for me anymore but he cares about me very much."

Jan, the Girlfriend

Jan and Mark met when she was 12 and he was 13. They, and other friends, spent several summers together. The two of them paired off soon after they met and they became pre-engaged the summer she turned 16. She says he never pressured her to have sex and she doesn't remember ever being asked.

When she turned 18, he gave her a diamond ring and they agreed to wait until both had finished college before getting married. She went to a local college and he went to an out-of-state university. When she found out that Mark was cheating on her with several different women, she confronted him. Mark first denied that he was cheating and then said that he was trying to learn as much as he could in order to be a better lover when he married her. He stressed that she needed to remain a virgin. She accepted his excuses until she learned that he was living with a girlfriend and she broke up with him and returned his ring.

"Eventually I married, and Mark contacted me... would I meet and give my approval for him to marry someone. He introduced me to Lisa, a very nice, naive girl, who reminded me of me at a much younger/innocent age. Mark confided that she was a virgin, and he was very proud of that fact. I gave my blessing, what did I care who he married? He married her and they had a daughter."

Alexia, the Wife

Alexia says despite her boyfriend calling her a whore once during their 18-month courtship, he was very attentive and bought her gifts and flowers. After they got married and their sex life began deteriorating she thought it was because of his tiring work schedule. Later, when their marriage began deteriorating, he *"admitted he saw me differently as soon as I became his wife—I wanted to have a normal relationship physically but it would only be on his terms and when he wanted it."*

A first pregnancy ended in a miscarriage; a daughter was born three years later. Three years after that, a second daughter was born. During her pregnancy her husband refused to be sexually intimate telling her "it's disgusting." She finally realized he didn't really want a physical relationship with her.

During the next few years he continued to avoid having a sexual relationship with her telling her that his perception of her as a woman had changed when they married and changed again when she became a mother. *"His words were: 'you don't do to your wife what you would do to just some bird you're shagging.'"* During a particularly heated argument he told her *"that he didn't love me, didn't want to be with me, and that if I didn't like the status quo I should go and get a divorce."*

"I then suggested counseling and even up until the evening of the appointment I didn't know if he was going to come along or not but off we went together for our first two-hour counseling session. It was at the end of that session that the counselor mentioned his 'Madonna/whore complex.' I immediately just knew exactly what she meant by it.

We came home and he thought she meant if I looked a little more like Madonna (the pop singer) he might fancy me more!! After about 10 days (and a second counseling session during which nothing was really achieved other than me getting very distressed) I Googled Madonna/whore complex and came across your description and identified straightaway that yes this is indeed what my husband has.

I held onto the information for about another ten days as I was really scared of the impact of this on him however I showed it to him and he started crying and saying sorry. I thought it was because he finally realized just how awful our marriage has actually been however in our final counseling session together he admitted that he'd been crying because he realized that he would never have what he really wants.

He has now been abusive and violent towards me and I have asked him to move out for my and the children's' safety—from here the only route is divorce."

Deb, the Girlfriend

Deb and Craig enjoyed spending time together but when Craig asked her how many men she had sex with prior to him, she admitted to having had sex with four men prior to meeting him. From that point, Craig wanted details about the men including their ages, penis size and sexual positions. She said: *"He even asked me, 'How could you f—k that guy? What attracted you to him?' Every day he would ask me invasive questions even while we were making love."* At one point he said she had *"whore qualities."*

"He calls a lot of women whores based on their 'situations.' He said that he hates all women except me because I'm 'different.' I suppose I am 'different from most women he's met.' I'm too nice and I'm very quiet. People insinuate that I'm virginal for some reason."

Deb and Craig took a trip to meet his family and during time they were apart he told her he had sex with a stranger he met at a gas station. He continued to cheat with random women he picked up at public places such as shopping malls.

"He even cheated on me with a woman who had a boyfriend. She knew he had a girlfriend. He justified it by saying she didn't love her boyfriend and that she only stayed with him for the children.

In her case, he said, she wasn't a whore. She was 'cool' and he mentioned that she had qualities that were like mine, whatever that means.

From what I gather and what my boyfriend has told me, he has a bad relationship with his mother. He doesn't talk to her and when he does, he embarrasses her in front of his family. His mom is a promiscuous woman. She is a very angry and hostile person."

Angela, the Wife

Angela and Rory abstained from sex during the three years they dated due to their strong Christian backgrounds. They have been married for just over a year. She says that Rory's mother is obsessed with teaching sexual abstinence to her kids due to her rushed marriage after becoming pregnant with Rory's older brother. She says Rory's parents are not affectionate people and describes his mother as a cold, frigid woman who has taught her children that sex is wrong.

"My husband when we were dating however was passionate, romantic, and more mature (five years older) telling me how lucky I was ('being so beautiful') that I didn't get in a relationship with a man who would have 'taken advantage' of me sexually.

So now we are past the first year of marriage, having sex once a week if we are lucky. I am constantly having to beg, which he claims is an 'unattractive turn off' and seems so 'desperate.' I will not initiate, and then STILL nothing will happen.

I am not an unattractive woman. I work out, eat healthy, and am constantly being hit on by attractive men. I have tried it all, lingerie, dirty talk (big mistake—that was 'slutty') you name it. He never wants me sexually.

On the outside, we have the perfect marriage, I am well educated, have good morals, I am fit and attractive, and he is likewise. But this secret of ours is tearing me apart. My self-confidence has never been lower, and I am ashamed to say that any man that pays attention to me becomes the object of some escapist sexual fantasy in my mind, because of our lack of intimacy.

Our marriage is wonderful on every other level, which makes this that much more painful. We both want the same things in life, and I know we love each other deeply. Love has never been the problem, which is why I feel guilty even complaining.

'You should feel lucky' my girlfriends will joke with me, 'my husband wants it all the time!' I laugh with them, but on the inside I am crying. Must be nice... what is wrong with me? Why doesn't my husband 'want it all the time' or even at all?! When we do, it feels like he is doing me a big favor.

I don't know where else to turn or what else to do... I feel like I am too young to be dealing with this, I am 21 years old, and my husband is 26.

He went to the doctor to get his testosterone levels checked, (begrudgingly because of my tearful pleas) and the doctor said he was normal, and even cracked jokes about his 'young wife's high libido!'

I am sick about this. I do not want a divorce. I want us to have as healthy as a sex life as we do in every other aspect."

Audrey, the Wife

"I am in a relationship with a man who is a textbook case of the Madonna whore complex. His mother was an alcoholic who worked in bars and was very promiscuous, and very detached from him. When I met him he was full of stories of his very manly exploits so much so that I teasingly called him a man-whore. We dated a long time with no touching whatsoever and finally I made the first move

which he went along with reluctantly. Sex never really increased with us even though I did become pregnant. During the pregnancy he would not touch me at all. Now, two years later, sex is rare. I try to discuss it, he becomes very angry. He has told me before to not ask for it, don't talk about it, don't initiate. He said women who are fast or flashy are a turn off. He told me I was a whore for wanting it.

I did have an affair and was caught. Because of our children he allowed me to stay in the home. Immediately after the affair, rather than reject me sexually, he went overboard. It was several times a day. He did things he would have never considered before. It was great and then as we slowly healed our relationship the sex stopped again. There is no foreplay, he won't kiss or cuddle and says the reason for that is because he was not raised in an affectionate family. He never knew his father and was raised by his absent mother and his sisters. I don't know if there is anything I can do to fix this. I feel horrible about myself and lost."

Juliet, the Wife

Juliet, a pretty and sensual girl, grew up in the 50's and 60's, coming of age during the sexual revolution. She was a "good girl" who didn't want to displease her mother who told her that sex was for marriage only and that girls who "did it" before marriage were "whores." She dated a lot and despite kissing and making out, she never would go "all the way" despite being called a prude, a lesbian, a cock-teaser. Because she refused to put out, boyfriend after boyfriend left her, and she never had a long-term boyfriend.

"The years went by. At 28 and still a virgin I met my future husband. This man must really love me, I thought, because not

going all the way didn't seem to bother him. He courted me and I remained a virgin. We married a week before I turned 30. I was so happy and ready to become a woman, be normal, and have real sex! Well, on our wedding night I was still a virgin and all during our honeymoon. It seemed he couldn't do it with me.

He always talked about how he was turned on by barmaids. I was very ladylike, far from a barmaid. He didn't seem to be turned on by me. But we both wanted children, a family. So by what I claim to this day was close to an immaculate conception, (he ejaculated around me, barely in me) I quickly became pregnant. The minute we found out he stopped going near me. When we wanted a second child it was the same thing. And then a third.

After the third baby my frustration and depression were all-consuming. But I had a young family to raise and this was my life. With three young children and a husband who traveled much of the time, I pretended to be a normal married woman. But I was sleeping alone in a closet of a room while he slept in the king-sized bed. Many times I tried to leave, but he told me I was selfish for wanting to break up a family because of sex. He also told me he would change. I never lost hope that one day he would want me and I would be a normal married woman.

The years passed. I remained a married virgin with three children. One day after we were married over 26 years he came to me and told me he couldn't change. He will let me go. I was 56 years old, lacking estrogen, the veteran of three C-sections and four hernia operations that left my belly slack and numb. Sex passed me by; it was never in my past and wouldn't be in my future.

Meanwhile, my sexless ex-husband started seeing a woman 10 years younger than me. They sleep and travel together. I've been told she is not pretty like me. The opposite of me, she is loud, drinks, smokes cigarettes and curses. This is his barmaid dream come true. The pretty wife he left behind is a madonna/virgin still.

One thing that confuses me just a little is that if indeed my husband suffered from the whore/madonna syndrome, it was also complicated by sexual dysfunction (premature ejaculation and eventually impotence). Sometimes I wonder which came first. He did, however, tell me many times during our courtship and early marriage that I looked like his mother (I looked nothing like his mother). He wanted me to wear my hair like hers. And when I started going gray he said he wouldn't mind if I didn't dye it. His mother was prematurely gray.

Also, after we separated he went into a sexual dysfunction treatment program. He told me at that time that he didn't want to be a 'eunuch' for the rest of his life. That really pained me when my youth had been wasted living with him the way he was."

The Husbands and Boyfriends

James, the Boyfriend

James, 28, recognized himself in my website article. He says that he has had a long and painful history of not being able to have any feeling of passion or a sexual relationship with women that he loves but he has no difficulty being very sexually active with numerous partners *"but rarely more than 3-4 times per partner. At that point I am usually too disgusted. I believe in some way it is a reflection of some subconscious self-hatred I feel for myself, that I become disgusted by the women I have conquested."*

He says that he is currently in a three-year relationship with the woman he knows he will marry and for the first 18 months he was able to *"sexualize her and take her like a man."* For the past 18 months he has been unable to feel passion for her and says *"Sex has for me become a matter of fantasizing about other women, projecting, masturbation and erectile enhancing pills."*

He recognizes that he has a problem but doesn't know how he can change.

"Maybe it's easier not to change and try to solve the M/W conundrum, but to reprogram me the way I see my girlfriend—

cast her as the whore. This might be easier to do (still not easy though). Then I could try to integrate the two, see her less as a madonna and more as an object of sexuality, somehow balance these two points of view until reaching what I hope will be a healthy medium.

Maybe more realistic since I'm not sure where I can find or who can provide me the tools to do it any other way. In any case 'curing' something like this sounds very 19th century, or even somewhat 21st century as in 'curing homosexuality.' Surely you are what you are and will enjoy more success by working with it rather than against it."

Pierre, the Boyfriend

Pierre, 39, says he has the Madonna/Whore Complex and that my article provided the best definition of the complex he's found so far. He says the problem is "pretty common" in Italy, where he lives.

"I've had hundreds of 'whores' in my life and a couple of 'Madonnas.' All my relationships have miserably failed, because of this problem. I also happen to have a good understanding of Psychology. I've read tons of books, but never really went to therapy.

How do I overcome this complex? Is there anything that I can do? Any advice at all? I'm tired to live this life with the two extreme of the equation (Madonna/whore), and long to be normal.

I know your book is supposed to help women, but what about men?? They are the cause of the problem, aren't they? Please, also, don't forget that we also are victims, because we absorb from society our beliefs."

Mike, the Boyfriend

Mike was born out of wedlock and raised by a single mother who had been sexually molested by her own father and came to view all men as rapists and/or pedophiles. She ended her two-year relationship with Mike's biological father when she became pregnant with Mike and didn't have another relationship with a man until he was fifteen.

Mike grew up with his mother constantly telling him that men were evil: his father, her father, molesting priests, men where she worked. At the same time she told him that he'd be different, he was a good boy. *"She wanted to make me into the ideal male,"* he wrote.

"I was a horny teenager loaded with shame and guilt because I was becoming what my mother despised, a man. I think I had three girlfriends before the age of twenty-two but none of them lasted more than a few weeks mainly because, a) none could live up to the ideal fantasy girl I'd made up in my head; b) I was ashamed of my body, because I'm a male (though I learned later in my twenties that I am somewhat of a hottie); c) the one time a girl I was crazy over and I were going to lose our virginity together, I made the mistake of consulting my mother—and she shamed me out of it.

So I ended up losing my virginity at twenty-two, in a very un-special way, to a girl I didn't know, and didn't care anything about. I played catch-up for the next eight years in a string of conquests that, upon further reflection, added up to sweet fuck all.

I have been in love four times. The longest of these relationships lasted approximately four months. Generally, the woman I fell for is beautiful, fairly intelligent, and vulnerable. Taught by my mother to be prince charming—she constantly recounted her childhood molestation/adult rape stories to me and I was supposed to console her—I often got involved with women that 'needed rescuing' (though I now understand that we all should work through our own crap instead of passing the buck).

Unfortunately, once a girl recounts, say, a bad sexual experience like rape to me, I will see the encounter unfold my head. There's nothing more soul-destroying than holding the girl you love while she's sobbing over what some other guy did. Because she's not the only one that's robbed—now I'm robbed, too.

I'd see that story run on and on in my head like a movie while I was at home, at work, at school, or trying to fall asleep at night. Or trying to have sex with her. In my mind, she's not mine, she's someone else's. Permanently. I can't explain it other than to say that it felt like a part of me was being violated. Like someone stealing something that belongs to me.

No. It's like waking up one morning to find out some punks stole your brand new car in the middle of the night, had a joy-ride in it all night, and you find your car the next morning with shattered windows, dents, hubcaps missing... Sigh. I'll take a taxi to work because I don't want anyone to see this embarrassment. I suppose the taxis are all the girls I fuck-n-chucked. No big investment, so nothing to lose.

In my mind, I've always hungered for the 'good girl,' like the Starship Enterprise where I could take 'where no man has gone before.' The kind of girl my mother always told me I should lose my virginity too (after we're married, of course). I've even had a few virgins but, as the Madonna Whore Syndrome explains, if they're too easy, I just lose interest.

At thirty-six, I've finally discovered that my mother probably has Borderline Personality Disorder, depression, anxiety, and throw in some narcissistic tendencies. She ensured I had no other adults to turn to for advice and support—I was to turn to her and her alone for advice and support. What a madhouse.

I've also discovered that I have BPD tendencies, depression, anxiety, and, apparently, Madonna Whore Syndrome. What an utter waste of a life.

Don't think I'm unsympathetic to the wrongs I've committed. I quit drinking and women four years ago (though the cigarettes, coffee, and porn have been harder to quit). I've tried to apologize to God. During this time, I've made an effort to view the women I know as friends—and I've slept with none of them. The problem is, I can't have more than a few beers without the fear of slipping up and I don't really know how to socialize—really socialize. I used to do it at the bar. Now, I'm a lonely internet addict."

Sam, the Husband

Sam was divorced after 24 years of what he called a long sexless marriage. He and his wife had three children. He says of his current relationship *"(I) love her to death and after a torrid sexual beginning with her, we are now sexless."* When he read my article about the Madonna/Whore Complex he wrote that the article *"sounds like me in many ways, with some differences."*

"I am NOT a jealous person, about her or anyone else. I am NOT controlling and wondering what her every move and action is. I still find my partner very attractive; I just can't find the drive. I remain 'faithful' in my relationship but fantasize about being with 'dirty' women, as stated in the article. I don't want things to be this way, but I see a pattern in my behavior. What treatments are available to help with this problem??"

There can be many things that will cause a lack of desire in a relationship. Sam needs to get a medical check-up to rule out physical or hormonal issues. If he gets a clean bill of health then he should make an appointment with a therapist who specializes in male sexual dysfunction so psychological reasons can be explored.

Eric, the Husband

Eric completed the contact form on my Madonna/Whore website and said he would be willing to tell his story for this book. A year passed before he contacted me again and asked if I was still looking for contributions and I told him I was. He said he would be willing to go into more detail about his feelings and experiences if I thought it would be useful. The following is his submission for this book — it has been edited for anonymity.

Dreams

There is so much I could write, however I have tried in the end to give the reader a taste, rather than a history of the continual internal and external conflicts that rage, with those that suffer from the so called whore Madonna complex. Some will accuse us of using psychobabble to permit immoral behavior, some are not able to reflect on their own weaknesses and humanity, some understand, but all get hurt, all are hurt, and all seek wholeness.

My memories, which are more like dreams of the world, both internal and external that I have inhabited for the last 4 or 5 years of my life have been confusing and dark, occasionally a beam of light has managed to break into these dreams, but in general darkness has ruled during this period. One of those times was the first experience I had with a prostitute. Looking back and understanding that I used another human being for my sexual needs, I feel mixed. On the one hand I need to feel the shame that this event generated within me, there are some times in life that it is important to experience such shame, other parts of me continues with the mentality of a victim and pays litter attention to this other person. There is the numb part of me that feels little about anything. Somewhere in the back ground there is healthy guilt, however due to the chronic neurotic guilt that I have experienced for much of my life, I am unable to tell the difference and hear this warning to my soul.

My mind plays games with even the word, is a woman in a massage parlor even a prostitute, surely she is not the same as someone standing on the side street in the hot autumn evening, showing leg and shoulder with the hope of winning a few dollars from the many young and old men, looking with leering anticipation.

It was a hot evening and I was again in a different city and country. For years I had been indulging in increasing amounts of internet pornography, cybersex and virtual cruising, but I had often vowed I would never ever actually go and meet somebody in person. The young Asian girl massaged me, it was all consuming and amazing, it was a dream, she had then asked me if I wanted sex, I said no, for some reason just a taste was enough. I negotiated a price for some teasing hand stimulation. I came. I put the present that I had bought my beautiful wife, in its bag on the side cabinet and forgot about it, until afterwards.

For the first time in my life I felt whole, this was me in my eyes at that time, being a man, who could turn women on, who could be the male that somehow had formed in my head as a picture of the perfect hero. Others would see a very different picture but to me it not only felt ultimately good, it was heaven on earth. Or at least it was for a moment, even though it was only for a moment, my worlds collided, and my life was not to be the same again. I left that place feeling not in heaven but in hell, my world imploded around me and I realized that the centre of control was no longer a matter of ambiguity; this "thing" had me. My wife at home with the children had no idea at this time, but now was the not the time to think about that. My wife was a saint; I only had been a devil in my mind. Yet there was another dynamic, a still voice, which I could ignore, but not make silent. This voice called me towards a journey of self discovery, one which I knew would ultimately bring me and others both health and pain.

Having vowed to never do this again and the constant tears that had accompanied me for my long flight evaporated that next evening, as I craved more than anything else in the whole world that feeling, that high once more.

This time it was an escort, an absolutely stunning girl from the slums of the city I was now in. The details I will leave to your imagination. Again, what would turn into a pattern for me, I did not engage in full sex. However I now no longer use this as a sort of justification, my engagement with this other person however sunk deeply into my psyche. This time I felt like a savior to this poor girl, however it was of course my Spirit's poverty that was being projected onto this beautiful woman. I spent much of my time counseling this woman, after the business had been dealt with. This itself is a strange irony. Why could I not have such a relationship with my wife? I had not yet even asked the question but in time this question would split my soul, why the whore and not the Madonna, and why a split anyway?

The following months and indeed years became fuzzy; I lead a double life, reflecting the internal chasm in my soul. I meet many women over the course of the next 3 years, each time vowing to stop each time repeating my behavior. I have never been able to describe feelings well. Over time I have developed a way of understanding my feelings by relating them to different kinds of weather. My dreams where filled with storms, cyclones, lightning's and snow, reflecting the turmoil and the desire for purity. But why did this happen to me, and why now. The questions started to hit my like the spray from an automatic weapon. I needed to listen to that voice to journey, adventure, and I felt in some way ultimately gain victory over the raging storm that was myself. In the worlds of Jesus I needed to come to a point where I could say, with authority... be still.

Memories

Even after years of psychoanalysis, psychiatric support, 12 step programs, strong medication, the raw pain of the divide between mind and soul, church support groups, depression, pain, psychiatric assessments etc which have been at times over whelming, I am only making slow progress. Even last night I slipped out of a hotel room and into the hands of a beautiful woman. I find now it is really difficult to get up again afterwards and try to move forward to purity, I sometimes fall into the feeling that this thing has me for good and the more I struggle the more I will become entangled.

My break ground is within the church. Sex is an area deep within the shadow of this part of the church. However before leveling criticism at the church, I believe that this is also true for the wider society. Most people, like angels perhaps, fear to tread into the world of human sexuality, its hues, beauty as well as its ugly raw power make it something that our technical and mechanistic mentality finds hard to understand or accept either in ourselves or others. This is I think reflected in our increasingly distant treatment of religion as it is perhaps the human experience that makes us most like the divine.

When did I realize that something was wrong? For the most part of my life I thought I had been the lucky one, my parents were not addicts, I understood that they loved me, I lived in a middle class community, I went to church and had privileges that many people who I would meet over the next few years could only dream about. If I had been aware the signs had probably been there for a long time, but I did not know what I was looking for. The anger I had experienced as a child, the isolation, the emotional expectations that were placed on, the needs of others were always more important than my own. But this was normal, wasn't it?

There were a couple of specific moments that had happened as my soul had unexpectedly opened up over the previous few years. One was a few months before I got married. I had taken my wife to a surprise weekend break at a resort. In our hotel one evening I was tired and had lied down on the bed for a few minutes. All of a sudden a personality (in psycho analysis speak a complex) was awakened, and I became a very different person. For the next 2 hrs, I spat sexual needs from my mouth in an excessive, explicit and totally out of control manner. I only had partial or perhaps very little control over myself during this experience. I felt nauseous, sweated profusely, in fact my fiancé sat next to me bathing my brow for most of this time. I only have a vague memory of it, but enough to know that it must have been very concerning; worrying and deeply upsetting for the woman I was due to get married to.

We tried to talk about it to our pastor and was told that it should remind us that evil is a reality. While I can understand this, maybe life could have been different had our pastor had the psychology training to understand what was happening and perhaps even to know what might be ahead of us, or at least a referral to a psychologist. I do not in any way blame this person; I am simply asking the question what if.

Another event I specifically remember was after getting married. It was in the very early days of my struggle with internet pornography and chat rooms and my mother was visiting us. We had gone out for something to eat and I was sitting in the cafe and all of a sudden this dark dread came over me, again. I convulsed inside, sweat literally poured off me and I began to shake. I did not really understand why this feeling had literally taken me over at this point, but looking back the proximity of my wife and my mother at a time I was extremely venerable was too much for me to hold together. The double Madonna brought out a psychic backlash and it was that evening I first paid for a computer sex service.

My wife is a very intuitive person by nature and although I was not conscious of the nearness of internal conflict I know that she was and it was her suggestion that I see a local counselor. I had an indistinct feeling that something was wrong, very wrong; I didn't really know what, but I regularly felt that I might be found out, or felt guilty about crimes I had not yet committed. I thought what would the world think, if suddenly I was the one in the news shots, what would my friends, would I have any friends, would they be interested in the reasons, what was going on inside me.

To be honest I had no idea, other than a vague image of a ball of string that was completely tangled and had formed a web. The psyche has a powerful ability to visualize itself, and struggling with what I thought was Irritable Bowl Syndrome for years, my insides where literally tired up in knots.

I went to the counselor and asked if I could speak to him, in my naivety I thought maybe a couple of sessions would sort it all out.

This therapeutic relationship developed over the next 3 years, before we moved out of state. I continued this work by phone for the first year of our stay in our new home, but there came a time when my counselor honestly felt that he could no longer help me and I would need more local support. It was at this point that the first mention of the whore Madonna complex was made to me. During the last three years, I had probably spent 1000s of hrs on the computer, using porn, indulging in chat rooms etc. What made it difficult is that I had no idea why I could not stop doing this.

My counselor helped me decide on the next course of action and it was at this point that I found myself entering psychoanalysis of the Jungian school. During the previous three years of counseling, things had basically got worse, the classic disorientation of doing counseling and expecting to improve was at first difficult, but I fell down a hole. When we moved, I went to a doctor who starting to prescribe antidepressants and for a few months I had a respite, but it was not long before the old feelings of something being desperately wrong returned.

It was a particularly dark time when we moved and I wrote the following poem which expresses my situation at the time:

Life is not working out, I seem to be spiraling and spiraling down and down
Grabbing where I can at the soft shiny polished surface of the rabbit hole
I wonder if the bottom will come today or tomorrow, but not, down and down
As is the case when hurtling, time stands still, or at least travels a little slower
How did I trip, to fall, so fast, the spirals, keep spiraling down and down
Must this fall end in a million pieces, spread around with a mantle of flesh
Or is this the requirement required a broken and contrite soul

You can't really break anything without dropping it down and down,
Spiraling, sometimes you wonder if you are falling or the floor is raising
To greet and meet you with a thud that might bring darkness forever and ever
Looking directly up, there is a faint dream, of light shining down and down
Even now, the beams race after the plummeting stone, teasing and touching

Maybe there is hope that the rules will change, gravity reverse, darkness to light
Perhaps somehow, the down and down, can be considered up and up,
Spiraling and spiraling and spiraling and spiraling, to the cross.

My feelings become more and more dark and negative, my relationship with my children, my wife, others and myself was becoming more and more destructive, my temper was extremely unstable, my mood swings intensified, the darkness became heavier and at times almost unbearable, On arriving home from another business trip I resumed frequenting strip bars, escorts, and prostitutes. It was the only thing that kept me going. I started to contemplate suicide

I cruised regularly looking for sexual adventure, I surfed the net, I spent thousands of hrs in a zone which can only be described as dream like, I was lucky not to be caught up in a police sting, or be in a wrong place at a wrong time, regularly going into drug houses realizing that I was touching a world that I knew very little about. I was once 'caught' by a cop, strangely he was an angel in disguise, or could have been, his voice was one of the most gracious and thoughtful I think I ever came across, he sent me on my way with a warning... one of course I did not heed.

Reflections

The therapy started by dealing with the crippling neurotic guilt I had over sex in general, As I got past the initial discussions, it was obvious that sexually I was a deeply unwell person, my understanding of what sex was colored deeply by my upbringing. A conjunction of sexual development and power differentials in my home life, lead me into BDSM and the need for pain from something that should be about joy. It was also wrapped by a church background that I think understands almost nothing about human sexuality, there are a few people within it that do, but they have *almost no voice or influence, and are thought by most heretics, yet their ministry is desperately needed. I was lucky enough, maybe blessed, to find them.*

I don't think my family had deeply reflected on this aspect of life either, or thought they had tried to explain the mechanics to me. It was the integration of this part of life with the rest of life, that had been hopeless messed up, inside a deep and dark complex had been growing for years, causing I think the split of my soul. Cancer is a very good metaphor here, the complex, or emotional cancer had penetrated my soul and split it, causing horrendous pain and suffering. But like many cancers it had grown silently and deadly. Little did I know I would spend the next years fighting it.

I do not see it as a coincidence that a little time into my therapy my mother was diagnosed with endometrial cancer, a somatic rejection of the womb, of the very cradle that brought me into existence. Of course this is speculation, but I have learnt that synchronicity should not be ignored. As I write these words my mother's battle is nearing the end and I have another battle raging in me as to how to process and engage with my family, who has no ability to comprehend the troubles that I have gone through. Sometimes I feel manipulated and cast out, but they do not know what they do, responding to their own emotional situation and culture and the way in which they were bought up. Yet my anger and pain is real.

I did once try to engage my family with my scenario, but they were not prepared to listen, believing that their parenting was flawless and whatever problem I had was my problem, there was nothing that they could do, the dragon stirred, my therapist warned me to put it back to sleep as quickly as possible. To hope is important but to realize that full awareness might never happen is a difficult but pragmatic approach. I feel now that one layer of the onion is stripped off, but there are other layers and I must in time travel further down into the psyche, to ensure that all the damage on the underside of my boat, the consciousness that travels on the sea of my sub conscious, that saves me from psychosis and to ensure that I can stop this generational curse stops with me.

It seems to me that the central question for people who experience this split, many of whom become addicted to sexualized behavior, as we struggle to bridge the divide in our souls, is do I suffer from an illness or not. Is the whore Madonna complex a symptom or the central problem?

The anima, as Carl Jung postulated was never meant to be split, literally this word means soul, but Jung saw it as the way in which the male psyche referenced the female world and indeed the collective psyche of mankind. It was the anima that would guide a man's reaction to women. If that complex was split, then this would destabilize man's ability to relate to women. I have found this a useful metaphor. This leads to an understanding of the whore Madonna complex as an illness and sex addiction as one of its symptoms. But let's go back even further, if there is such a thing as an anima, why does it split? Are there alternative models to that of an illness? The implications for the future of how we deal with these scenarios within our society rest upon the answer to this question.

Can the Madonna/Whore Complex Be Cured?

This complex isn't fixed or "cured" the same as an illness or a physical condition would be. It is based on experiences and/or beliefs ingrained when the man was quite young, perhaps even in infancy or earlier. For there to be a positive change in his current beliefs, he must want to change and be motivated to do the work necessary in order to treat all women as whole persons—both good *and* bad—not as "either/or" entities.

It takes a medical professional who understands the complex (some don't) to diagnose the Madonna/Whore Complex. Unless a man is willing to admit that he has a problem, and seeks professional help to change his views of women, nothing will change. Some men with this complex aren't willing to admit they might have a problem even when it's the cause of their marriages failing.

Let's break this complex down to what it actually is: male marital sexual impotence. I think that term accurately describes the major issue of most men with this dysfunction.

Author Stephen A. Mitchell in *Can Love Last? The Fate of Romance Over Time* writes:

...Sigmund Freud asserted that "psychical impotence" was second only to anxiety as a form of neurotic distress in patients of his time. What he meant by psychical impotence was twofold. He was referring to impotence with psychological rather than physical causes. A man might be functionally potent in some circumstances but not in others: the problem was not in the equipment itself, but in his mind. But Freud was also referring to an impairment that did not necessarily manifest itself only in purely physical terms. In using "impotence" metaphorically, Freud was pointing to a psychosexual inhibition, a constraint in the capacity to arrive at and sustain desire itself, a kind of psychological flaccidity. A man might be capable of performing the physical act, going through the motions, but without passion, without intense desire.

A woman, even if she isn't "in the mood" for sex can fake it because she has no sex organ that gives her lack of passion away. A man's passion and readiness for sex is obvious; his penis can't lie. When a man is unable to feel sexual passion for the woman he loves, he won't be able to get or maintain an erection and he will be impotent. Even if impotence is never a factor in his other sexual encounters, the impotence he suffers with his wife is a very real condition.

No man wants to believe he's impotent and that's a big roadblock when trying to treat the Madonna/Whore Complex. The man needs to understand that there is a psychological cause for his impotence, and he needs to find a therapist who understands both the cause and potential cures. If he is able to get and maintain an erection with women other than his wife but cannot get and maintain an erection with her, he can stop worrying that there's a problem with his penis; the problem is buried deep in his subconscious. He also needs to push past any guilt he might feel; the root cause of the dysfunction occurred when he was too young to protect himself from its influence.

It's more difficult to diagnose and treat impotence problems that are "in your mind"—such as the Madonna/Whore Complex—than it is to treat physical problems caused by low testosterone, diseases such as diabetes, or other fairly easily identifiable issues. Doctors are more comfortable treating physical conditions; success is easy to determine. It's much more difficult to know if treatment for a psychological problem is making the problem better or if the treatment is causing another layer of stress and additional performance failure.

If a man is impotent with every woman he's intimate with there are medications and treatments that his doctor can prescribe. When he's only impotent with one woman he needs help learning why that woman isn't sexually stimulating to him.

In *Sexuality and the Psychology of Love,* Freud writes:

> We are accustomed confidently to promise recovery to psychically impotent patients who come to us for treatment; but we ought to be more guarded in making this prognosis so long as the dynamics of the disturbance are unknown to us. It comes as a disagreeable surprise if the analysis reveals the cause of the "merely psychical" impotence to be a typically masochistic attitude, perhaps deeply embedded since infancy.

According to information in the *Handbook of Sexual Dysfunction (Medical Psychiatry Series)(v. 30),* low male sexual desire can be either lifelong/situational or acquired/generalized. The Madonna/Whore Complex falls under lifelong/situational and the history, etiology, and treatment are shown as:

History: Desire present: when alone (masturbation, fantasy); at start of past relationship; desire decreases as relationship becomes more intimate.

Etiology: Interaction difficulty may manifest as Madonna/Prostitute Syndrome, or as Internet sexuality problem, or as "sexual addiction" (paraphilia-related disorder PRD)

Treatment: Individual and/or group psychotherapy.

Adultery will destroy a marriage even if there is no sexual dysfunction causing stress between the husband and wife. A wife already stressed over her husband's lack of desire for her, who learns that her husband has been unfaithful, may decide that divorce is her only option. In their book *Not "Just Friends": Rebuilding Trust and Recovering Your Sanity After Infidelity* authors Shirley P. Glass and Jean Coppock Staeheli write:

> Some men become constricted sexually with their wives after the first child is born because their exciting sex partner has now become a mother. An unfaithful husband sent sexually explicit greeting cards to his affair partner but never considered sending something like that to his wife. Even after his wife told him she would enjoy receiving a sexy card from him, he said, "I couldn't send something like that to you. You're my wife and the mother of my children."

Adultery is also the theme in this passage from Marion Woodman's book *Dancing in the Flames*:

> In his many affairs, James was acting out the virgin/whore split in his psyche. He needed the comfort and security of his wife/mother, and was anxious that she might reject him. At the same time, he was unable to express his lust to his wife/mother (virgin). In taking up a mistress (whore), he was providing himself with a stand-in as well as a stand-by; he now had someone to project his lust onto, and should wife/mother leave him, mistress would provide him with the comfort and security he needed. For James, as for most men, this split was rooted in the mother

complex. This highly charged complex carries with it the need for acceptance, comfort, security, and nurturance, and, at the same time, the fear of rejection, denial, destruction, and death. It sets a man upon the knife edge between womb and tomb. Dependence and fear create a psychic impotence that generates deep unconscious rage. This rage is at the crux of the patriarchal position.

In her book *Men Who Can't Be Faithful: How to Pick Up the Pieces When He's Breaking Your Heart*, author Carol Botwin writes:

It is difficult for a married man who suffers from the Pedestal/ Gutter Syndrome to remain faithful, because the wife either loses erotic interest in his eyes, or he arrives at the same place through a different unconscious maneuver. He chooses for a wife someone who conforms to the "good girl" image by not being very interested in sex. Either way, he feels that he is forced to look elsewhere for what he needs, often blaming it on the wife.

For a man to overcome the negative patterns of the Madonna/Whore Complex, he must be highly motivated and willing to put in the work necessary to find the root cause of his dysfunction; it is equally important that his wife be supportive throughout the therapy. Lifelong beliefs are difficult to eradicate and not every man will be able to overcome his negative programming which is why some therapists focus on helping the man, and his wife, to adapt their relationship accordingly.

If you're married to a man diagnosed with the Madonna/ Whore Complex or you think he has this sexual dysfunction, you already know that your marriage is in trouble. No two people deal with marital problems of this type in the same way so there is no single "cure all" or simple answer. Only you know whether you can give up—or want to give up— sexual intimacy in your marriage.

A man might be "cured" of this complex if he was willing to spend the time in therapy to reprogram his thinking but not every man with this complex believes he has a problem. Even if a man does go into therapy, it may not produce the results his wife is hoping for. My husband spent years in therapy apparently learning that he didn't have a problem, I did.

So what do you do? You're sexually frustrated and getting more hostile by the day over his lack of concern about your intimacy needs. Maybe he won't admit there's a problem or perhaps you're too inhibited to initiate a frank conversation with him about sex. Or maybe you've just discovered that he has a girlfriend, and she's not the first one since you've been married.

In their book *Rekindling Desire: A Step by Step Program to Help Low-Sex and No-Sex Marriages*, sex and marital experts Barry and Emily McCarthy write about the importance of sexual intimacy in marriage:

> Sexuality is a positive, integral component of marital intimacy. Although no-sex or low-sex marriage can function satisfactorily, these are the minority. Some couples maintain a respectful, trusting bond and are good parents even though sexuality is dysfunctional or absent. Other couples have an angry, alienated, nonsupportive marriage, and the only thing that works is sex.
>
> The most common pattern is a couple that has a good relationship, but struggles unsuccessfully with inhibited desire. Over time, the sexual problem becomes severe and chronic. Sexual problems undermine marriages by robbing them of intimate connection and energy.

I was married almost 16 years, virtually all of those years fitting into a no-sex category. Neither of us wanted to be parents so sex for procreation was out and we didn't have children to bind us or parenting duties to bond us. We had few common interests before and during marriage. Whatever intimate connection we may have had before marriage, we lost once we were married. Eventually there was absolutely nothing in our relationship to make me want to stay in it; he, on the other hand, was content with things as they were. My situation isn't the case in some marriages and the decision to stay or go will be more difficult than mine was.

The entire length of our marriage, my husband chose to ignore my sexual needs and satisfy his elsewhere. Even after he went into therapy there was no positive change in our relationship or the way he approached me sexually. The more sexually frustrated I became, the more I disliked him. I don't know what transpired in the therapy sessions that spanned the last ten years of our marriage although he was able to get his alcoholism under control and quit smoking. With regard to the Madonna/Whore Complex, his therapy sessions apparently focused on making him feel good about himself as he was; after all, he wasn't impotent and he certainly did like women—if there was a problem, it was mine to deal with.

Sexual dysfunctions are embarrassing to discuss and there might be a bit of a bias when a male doctor is treating a patient whose wife is complaining that the man is unable to function in the bedroom, and men make up the group therapy sessions. The man appreciates pretty women, likes boobs and butts, and can easily get an erection. What's the problem? *He* seems to be normal; perhaps the problem is something at home. In dealing with the Madonna/Whore Complex, there *is* a problem at home: his sexually frustrated wife.

Some marriages with this complex do work because each person's needs are being met within the relationship. In *Why Good People Do Bad Things: Understanding Our Darker Selves*, author James Hollis discusses the marriage between a man with the Madonna/Whore complex and his wife:

> So we have a second person in this pas de deux, called marriage, that has a Shadow issue. Edward and Emily were drawn together in the first place because they mirrored each other. Generally speaking, people are drawn toward intimate relationships either because they are opposites who will compensate each other, or because they are complementary, which means that not only their conscious likes and dislikes line up, but their complexes as well. Edward and Emily found each other because they were both walled off from their Eros. Edward had the need to put Emily on the pedestal because he suffered from a variant of the virgin/whore complex, an intrapsychic imago that separates and elevates "the feminine" into its celestial adoration, or delimits her through only her carnal form. This is the deep wedge that mother and priest managed to drive into the soul of this child.
>
> Emily, on the other hand, had a similar history and cultural influence, and so had a strong need to be on that pedestal.

If the man is unable or won't make an effort to change, the woman married to a man with this complex can try to sublimate her intimacy needs and focus on other aspects of her marital relationship or her life in general. I was able to focus on my career, and various hobbies, with an intensity I might not have had otherwise.

She also might try to make herself more sexually attractive to him. His reaction, if he does have this complex, will make her feel even less attractive and desirable. After a couple extremely embarrassing attempts to turn myself into the sultry temptress my husband *said* I needed to be in order to excite him, I was too demoralized to try again which had probably been his intention from the beginning.

Some women take a lover to validate their self-worth and attractiveness. Adultery is never an answer to a marital problem but divorce can be.

If you're married to a man with this complex, and he's not willing or trying to change, it's a "ball in your court" situation. This is how life will be with him. Can you accept it? Are his other qualities worth staying in a sexually unfulfilling marriage? Is everything else in your relationship a good enough trade-off for the lack of sexual intimacy?

He does love you—that's why he doesn't want to "dirty" you with the sex act. If he was to fall out of love with you, he would treat you as he would any whore and he would be able to have sex with you. If he fell back in love, he would again treat you as the woman he loves—and his sexual passion for you would be gone again.

Can you live without sexual intimacy with him or anyone else for the rest of your life?

Can you pleasure yourself when he's not around in order to at least get sexual release when you need it? For the rest of your life?

If he isn't having sex with you, is he getting sex elsewhere? Can you live with that?

Sex to him is dirty. *We* know that it is a beautiful experience when shared with someone we love. He may never be able to get past his programming so that he regards sex as a necessary part of a loving relationship. Can you accept this and regain positive feelings about yourself?

You are not a horrible person for wanting a normal sex life with the man you love. And he is not a horrible person for having dysfunctional sexual beliefs. This is a painful situation for both of you.

Take a long look at your entire relationship with him. Is there abuse, addictive behavior, or other negative aspects that make this a relationship that would be tenuous even if there were no problems with sexual intimacy?

I don't have answers, just a lot of questions you need to answer as *you* figure out the future you want for *you*.

Trying to find a reason for your marriage to be in such trouble might be a waste of time and energy and you might be looking in the wrong direction for answers. Some questions I'd be asking would be:

1) How long did you date before getting married?

2) Were you a virgin and/or very sexually inexperienced when he met you?

3) Is this your first marriage? It's unlikely that a man with this complex would marry a divorced woman simply because of her sexual experience in the prior marriage.

4) Has he ever been married before and if so, why did that marriage end?

5) What type of relationship does he have with his mother?

6) Is he in a long-term affair or has he had several short-term affairs?

If you need help making decisions, you might want to search for a therapist or marriage counselor in your area. If you suspect the Madonna/Whore complex is a part of the marital problem, be sure to ask any counselor you're considering if they have experience in the issue.

Common behaviors of "average" men with the Madonna/ Whore complex:

1) Even though he may be very sexually experienced, he only wants to marry someone who is a virgin when he begins dating her.

2) If he discovers that his "virginal" girlfriend has had sex with someone else, she is moved to the "whore" category and is no longer someone he wants to marry but she might be someone he'll continue to have sex with.

3) He can be quite sexually active with his inexperienced/ virginal girlfriend but marriage and the birth of a child or children help to solidify his view of her as the pure Madonna who he would never want to soil by the dirty act of sex. Even if they don't have children, he won't want to degrade her by having sex with her.

Again, referring to Elvis Presley, he met Priscilla when she was a young teen, tried to turn her into a mirror image of his mother in looks, and (according to what Priscilla writes in her book) didn't care to have sex with her after their child was born. He had many affairs throughout his life, even when he was married.

No one else can tell you whether it's better to stay in a sexless marriage or to get out of it. You have to weigh the good and the bad and make the decision that's best for you. Walking away from my marriage was one of the most joyous events in my life; I had never felt as free in my entire life. Your relationship with your husband may be much stronger and more loving than mine was; that makes your decision more difficult and I don't envy your struggle to do the right thing.

As a final note, I asked one of the women whose story appears in this book what advice she would give to someone married to a man with the Madonna/Whore Complex. This was her response:

"It's all about truth and self-esteem. If you believe that a vital part of marriage is intimacy and affection and you experience the poison when that is lacking, then you will have the strength to admit to a mistake and seek the life you deserve. Young people should be taught this.

I wish I could go back. I can't. Women must understand that men do not change. If something feels so wrong, it is wrong. Get out when you're still young. Never be with someone who doesn't desire you in every way. Passion may change throughout the years, but if you feel that your partner is turned off in any way by you and working together doesn't help this feeling, then you must leave.

If it is not meant to be that you be loved by a man, then you must love yourself. And you cannot love yourself, if you have submitted to indifference or worse."

The Dark Side of the Madonna/Whore Complex

In very rare cases the Madonna/Whore Complex may be an underlying cause when a man takes out his aggression on women for the perceived wrongs he suffered early in life. I'm not trying to imply that all men who suffer from the Madonna/Whore Complex are abusive, rapists, stalkers, or potential serial killers—that's far from the truth. I'm including this information in order to provide everything about this complex I have been able to find.

In his book *The Macho Paradox: Why Some Men Hunt Women and How All Men Can Help,* author Jackson Katz writes about misogynistic attitudes of some men that result in violence to women:

> ...*Many women who strip are also prostitutes, but in the minds of many men, there is not a big difference between the two. The good girl/bad girl dichotomy is alive and well, and when a woman is a bad girl, some men who have been socialized in our deeply misogynistic culture believe she is no longer worthy of their respect. In fact, when a woman so much as takes her clothes off in public, some men think she has given up her right to control when and with whom she wants to have sex.*

From *Pornified: How Pornography Is Damaging Our Lives, Our Relationships, and Our Families*:

... Rather than a mark of escape from the past, the dominant morality of pornography reeks of Puritan and Victorian prudery; it creates a world populated by virgins and whores, by women who are used and shamed for being sexually voracious. Their degradation is deserved, according to the prime sexual vision of the pornographer. Even when the woman isn't overtly degraded, she is deemed less than the man watching her by dint of being paid to please him sexually in a public forum ... In pornography, sexuality frequently accompanies or provokes disgust and hatred—something to be done quickly, and just as quickly disposed of. In the world of pornography, sex is generally dirty, cheap, and—in the end—not much fun.

The following excerpt is from a paper titled "The Archetypes and Psychodynamics of Stalking," written by Glen Skoler, Ph.D., included in *The Psychology of Stalking: Clinical and Forensic Perspectives*:

Freud (1953), of course, immediately recognized a repressed oedipal theme in the rescuing the whore fantasy. By this theory the prostitute is a mother figure imagined to be degraded and defiled in acts of sexuality with a powerful, potent father figure, and is perceived (with ambivalent anger and idealization) as a victim who needs to be rescued, in the jealous eyes of the adoring, but sexually immature, male child. Beyond the Freudian interpretation this fantasy is probably so archetypal because it is overdetermined. Themes of rescuing the whore can condense and coalesce several oedipal and pre-oedipal psychodynamics.

The predictable Freudian interpretation, however, helps to explain the counterintuitive paradox: why some erotomanic and obsessional stalkers—who often have rather inadequate heterosexual skills and histories—become obsessed with imagined "whores" and sexual sophisticates such as film stars— women who are perceived as sexually experienced, and threatening, to an obviously fragile and inadequate male ego. However, part of the imagined happy ending of the fantasy is that the union with the "whore" will be a highly idealized pure and spiritual love, devoid of the supposedly degrading and "dirty" sexuality she is expected to cease with other women. Choosing unattainable love objects, such as celebrities, also insulates the stalker from the threat of actual sexual contact.

Author David D. Gilmore in his book *Misogny: The Male Malady* explains why a man might feel a need to degrade his sex partners:

Freud starts with the plausible proposition that many men never resolve their Oedipal feelings toward the mother and, as a consequence, suffer lifelong sexual dysfunction because they are unable to accept a sexual woman as distinct from mother. For such a conflicted man, later sexual life is distorted by psychic associations of eros with the incestuous object of childhood, the child's primary choice object (1912:180). For such a conflicted man, sex always remains illicit, incestuous, and frightening, for he regards the sexual act basically as something degrading, "which defiles and pollutes not only the body" but also the spirit (1912:186).

In order to obtain erotic release, therefore, these neurotic, sexually conflicted men must demean the sexual object. By doing so they compartmentalize their sex lives and rescue the mother (1910:168) from the pollution of their own Oedipal cravings. Thus, all potential sexual partners in adult life — that is, all nubile and unrelated women — must be denigrated as "worthless" and "dirty." This debasement of sexual function goes hand in hand with an overvaluation — in fact, idolization — of the mother as pure and sexless, and therefore the exact opposite of a sexual woman. And thereby is enacted a psychic contrast and separation of love objects, the psychic "splitting" between mother and sexual partner that gives rise in cultural terms to the madonna-whore complex of Catholic Europe and the good girl-bad girl double standard of Victorian morality, with all the misogynistic stereotyping that must inevitably ensue from such a dichotomous vision.

Was the Madonna/Whore Complex a factor in the killing of prostitutes by the elusive "Jack the Ripper"? The killer was never caught or identified, so there is no way to know what motivated the killings or even if the killer was a man—although a man was seen running from the scene of one of the murders. Because prostitutes were the targets and the crimes were so vicious it seems to indicate that the killer had more than a casual interest in destroying these types of women.

Mike DeBardeleben may have been one of the most prolific serial killers the U.S. has ever known. Author Katherine Ramsland, in her article for TruTV.com *Mike DeBardeleben: Serial Sexual Sadist*, writes this about DeBardeleben's childhood:

> *DeBardeleben was born on March 20, 1940 in Little Rock, Arkansas, the middle of three children. He was named after his father, who was an army officer and a rigid, controlling autocrat with a bad temper. Young Mike apparently had a strong love-hate relationship with his mother, who was an alcoholic and who frequently punished him for his stubbornness. By the time he was in high school, he had started to beat her up. He also got caught with a weapon and by the age of 16, racked up his first arrest. He went into the military but was quickly court-martialed for a variety of offenses.*

When FBI agents searched DeBardeleben's home after he was arrested on counterfeiting charges, the agents found evidence of multiple sexual-sadism crimes against women including murder. He faced prosecution in nine states and by the time six trials were over he was facing 375 years in jail in addition to two life sentences; the exact victim count may never be known.

In his book *Beyond Cruel,* author Stephen G. Michaud, who had access to the FBI's files on DeBardeleben and had contact with him when DeBardeleben was in prison writes:

> *If Mrs. Macdonald did in fact resemble his mother, then you'd want to ask if there was a period in DeBardeleben's life when his father was unavailable, which there was. Did mother bring home a succession of drunken 'uncles' to share her bed? Was DeBardeleben exposed to his mother as slut and develop this notion that's called the whore-Madonna complex? 'Sluts like mother must die'? You look for that in prostitute killers.*

When they kill women, are some serial killers symbolically killing their own mothers? In *Sexual Murder: Catathymic and Compulsive Homicides,* author Louis B. Schlesinger writes:

> *Support is fairly widespread for the general notion that some men emotionally split women into sexual objects they view as bad, and non-sexual objects they view as good or pure. For example, Freud (1910) described a need in some men to degrade women in order to experience sexual arousal: "pure" women, whom they do not degrade, reflect the image of a mother, and create in these men sexual inhibitions and anxiety associated with incest. Mathis (1971) reported some extreme cases of this phenomenon, which he referred to as the "Madonna-prostitute" syndrome. Here, a man loses potency after marriage—or after his wife gives birth to a child—frequently insists that his spouse utter profanities during intercourse or admit to or describe details of other sexual encounters and indiscretions. If she does, the man is able to become aroused. The perceived "purity" of the wife (or new mother) generates too much incest anxiety. Revitch and Schlesinger (1981) postulated that in the compulsive murderer "the bad mother is either eliminated in totality, or she is split into a good mother (in the fantasy life) and a bad mother, or mother-prostitute, that deserved to be eliminated."*

Son of Sam killer David Berkowitz tried to fool prosecutors into believing that he killed because a talking dog instructed him to kill. In the book *Whoever Fights Monsters: My Twenty Years Tracking Serial Killers for the FBI*, by Robert K. Ressler and Thomas Schachtman, Ressler, who coined the phrase "serial killer" in 1978, details Berkowitz' early adoption, the death of his adoptive mother when he was fourteen, and his disappointment that his birth mother didn't want to make him a part of her family after he was able to locate her when he returned from a stint in the Army. Ressler writes:

> By the time I interviewed him, Berkowitz also had done enough talking with psychiatrists and other counselors in prison to be somewhat comfortable conversing about the true basis for his crimes. He admitted that his real reason for shooting women was out of resentment toward his own mother, and because of his inability to establish good relationships with women.

And, this excerpt from *Mind Hunter: Inside the FBI's Elite Serial Crime Unit* by John Douglas and Mark Olshaker:

> When my sister, Arlene, was a teenager, my mom used to say she could tell a lot about the boys Arlene was going out with by asking them how they felt about their mothers. If the boy professed love and respect for his mother, that would probably reflect his relationships with other women in his life. If he thought of his mother as bitch or whore or ball-buster, chances were pretty darn good he'd end up treating other women the same way.
>
> From my experience, my mom's observation was right on the money. Ed Kemper cut a trail of destruction through Santa Cruz, California, before he finally worked up the nerve to kill the one woman he truly hated. Monte Rissell, who raped and murdered five women as a teenager in Alexandria, Virginia, told

us that if he had been allowed to go with his father instead of his mother when their seriously troubled marriage broke up, he thought he'd be a lawyer now rather than a lifer at the Richmond Penitentiary, where we interviewed him.

Sources

"The Archetypes and Psychodynamics of Stalking," by Glen Skoler, Ph.D., in *The Psychology of Stalking: Clinical and Forensic Perspectives*, edited by J. Reid Meloy, Academic Press, 2001.

Attachment in Adulthood, Structure, Dynamics, and Change, by Mario Mikulincer, PhD, and Phillip R. Shaver, PhD, The Guilford Press, 2010.

Becoming Attached: First Relationships and How They Shape Our Capacity to Love, Robert Karen, Oxford University Press, 1998.

Beyond Cruel, by Stephen G. Michaud, St. Martin's True Crime, 2007.

The Body Project: An Intimate History of American Girls, by Joan Jacobs Brumberg, Vintage, 1998.

Bonds of Fire: Rekindling Sexual Rapture, by Alice Rose, Ph.D., 1996.

Can Love Last? The Fate of Romance over Time, by Stephen A. Mitchell, W.W. Norton & Company, 2003.

"Clinical Assessment in the Treatment of Sexual Dysfunctions," by W. Charles and Gretchen K. Lobitz in *Handbook of Sex Therapy (Perspectives in Sexuality)*, ed. Joseph LoPiccolo and Leslie LoPiccolo. Springer, 1978.

Clinical Manual of Sexual Disorders, by Richard Balon and Robert Taylor Segraves, American Psychiatric Publishing, Inc., 2009.

The Clintons Meet Freud: A psychohistory of Bill, Hillary and Chelsea, by Paul Loweringer, Knoll Press, 2004.

Dancing in the Flames, by Marion Woodman, Shambhala, 1997.

Elvis and Me, by Priscilla Beaulieu Presley, Berkley; Revised edition 1986.

Falling in Love: Why We Choose the Lovers We Choose, by Ayala Malach, Routledge; 2nd edition, 2005.

Freud and Beyond: A History of Modern Psychoanalytic Thought, by Stephen A. Mitchell and Margaret J. Black, BasicBooks, A division of HarperCollins Publishers, Inc.,, 1996.

"Freud's psychology and its organic foundation: Sexuality and mind-body interactionism," by B. Silverstein, *Psychoanalytic Review,* 72:203–228.

Handbook of Sexual Dysfunction (Medical Psychiatry Series)(v. 30), by Richard Balon and R. Taylor Segraves, Informa Healthcare; 1 edition, 2005.

He's a Stud, She's a Slut, and 49 Other Double Standards Every Woman Should Know, by Jessica Valenti, Seal Press, 2008.

If Men Could Talk: Unlocking the Secret Language of Men, by Alon Gratch, Little, Brown and Company, 2002.

"Impotence as a Practical Problem," by John Reckless and Nancy Geiger in *Handbook of Sex Therapy (Perspectives in Sexuality),* ed. Joseph LoPiccolo and Leslie LoPiccolo. Springer, 1978.

The Macho Paradox: Why Some Men Hunt Women and How All Men Can Help, by Jackson Katz, Sourcebooks, 2006.

Maiden USA: Girl Icons Come of Age, by Kathleen Sweeney, Peter Lang, 2008.

Mary: A Flesh-and-Blood Biography of the Virgin Mother, by Lesley Hazleton, Bloomsbury USA, 2005.

Masters and Johnson on Sex and Human Loving, by Robert Kolodny, Virginia E. Johnson, and William H. Masters, Little, Brown and Company, 1998.

Men Who Can't Be Faithful: How to Pick Up the Pieces When He's Breaking Your Heart, by Carol Botwin, Warner Books, 1988.

"Mike DeBardeleben: Serial Sexual Sadist," by Katherine Ramsland for TruTV. com.

Misogny: The Male Malady, by David D. Gilmore, University of Pennsylvania Press, 2001.

The Moral Animal: Why We Are, the Way We Are: The New Science of Evolutionary Psychology, by Robert Wright, Vintage, 1995.

Not "Just Friends": Rebuilding Trust and Recovering Your Sanity After Infidelity, by Shirley P. Glass and Jean Coppock Staeheli, Free Press, 2004.

Pornified: How Pornography Is Damaging Our Lives, Our Relationships, and Our Families, Pamela Paul, Holt Paperbacks, 2008.

Practicing Catholic, by James Carroll, Mariner Books, 2010.

The Purity Myth: How America's Obsession with Virginity Is Hurting Young Women, by Jessica Valenti, Seal Press, 2009.

Rekindling Desire: A Step by Step Program to Help Low-Sex and No-Sex Marriages, by Barry and Emily McCarthy, Routledge, 2003.

Secret Lives of Great Authors, by Robert Schnakenberg, Quirk Books, 2008.

Sexuality and the Psychology of Love, Sigmund Freud, Touchstone, 1997.

Sexual Murder: Catathymic and Compulsive Homicides, Louis B. Schlesinger, CRC Press, 2003.

Sex Work: Writings by Women in the Sex Industry, by Priscilla Alexander and Frederique Delacoste, Cleis Press; 2nd Edition, 1998.

Sexy Origins and Intimate Things: The Rites and Rituals of Straights, Gays, Bis, Drags, Trans, Virgins, and Others, by Charles Panati, Diane Pub Co. 1998.

Shrinking History: On Freud and the Failure of Psychohistory, by David E. Stannard, Oxford University Press USA, 1982.

"Sigmund Freud and His Impact on Our Understanding of Male Sexual Dysfunction," by Ume Hartmann in *The Journal of Sexual Medicine,* June 2009.

Theories of Attachment: An Introduction to Bowlby, Ainsworth, Gerber, Brazelton, Kennell, and Klaus, by Carol Garhart Mooney, Redleaf Press, 2009.

A Virgin Conceived: Mary and Classical Representations of Virginity, by Mary F. Foskett, Indiana University Press, 2002.

Why Good People Do Bad Things: Understanding Our Darker Selves, by James Hollis, Gotham, 2008.

Yes Means Yes: Visions of Female Sexual Power and a World Without Rape, by Jessica Valenti and Jaclyn Friedman, Seal Press, 2008.

About the Author

PAT GAUDETTE is an author, publisher, and website developer. She is the author of *How to Survive Your Husband's Midlife Crisis: Strategies and Stories From the Midlife Wives Club; Journaling through His Midlife Crisis: Redefining Your Life As He Reinvents His; Teen Mom: A Journal; How to Be a Self-Published Author: A Step-by-Step Guide; Advice for an Imperfect Single World; Advice for an Imperfect Married World; Midnight Confessions: True Stories of Adultery;* and *Sparky the AIBO: Robot Dogs & Other Robotic Pets.*

She is the founder/webmaster of popular relationship-oriented websites including *The Midlife Club* (MidlifeClub.com) and the award-winning *Friends and Lovers the Relationships Guide* (FriendsandLovers.com). She and her husband live in Florida.

Email her at: pat@halpi.com

Visit her website: www.patg.com

How to Survive Your Husband's Midlife Crisis: Strategies and Stories from The Midlife Wives Club

Authors: Pat Gaudette & Gay Courter
Home & Leisure Publishing, Inc.
ISBN 978-0-9825617-5-1
Available in Paperback, Kindle
& eBook Versions

You've heard all the jokes about men's midlife crises – the new sports car, the new exercise regimen... and the new girlfriend. But when you're the wife trying to cope, it's no laughing matter.

A midlife crisis can devour a relationship. It may be devouring yours. The Midlife Wives Club is a supportive sisterhood for midlife mates – a chance to vent some steam, share advice, or just get a reminder that you're not alone. In this guide, you'll find wisdom from both midlife wives and experts on:

•Recognizing the symptoms
•Coping with the threat (or reality) of infidelity
•Identifying underlying problems like depression and anger
•Deciding when to stick it out – and when to pack it in
•Protecting your kids from the fallout
•Making it through the crisis... and coming out stronger, saner, and more self-reliant

With personal stories from real women (and men) and a comprehensive list of resources, **How to Survive Your Husband's Midlife Crisis** can help you get past the rough spots – and turn this tumultuous time into a change for the better.

Available in paperback as well as eBook and Kindle versions through Amazon.com and other retailers.

For immediate support for midlife issues visit www.MidlifeClub.com.

Teen Mom: A Journal

Edited by: Pat Gaudette
Home & Leisure Publishing, Inc.
ISBN 978-0976121084
Available in Paperback, Kindle
& eBook Versions

Sixteen-year-old "Katie" was half way through her junior year of high school when she became pregnant. Throughout her pregnancy and for several months afterward, she kept a journal. This is her story as told in that journal.

Katie is not one teenager dealing with unplanned pregnancy, she is one of many. She may be the girl next door or the girl in the next block. She may be your daughter. She may be you.

Teens are more openly sexually active than in past generations and unplanned pregnancy is not the social stigma of years ago. The pregnancy of pop idol Britney Spears' 16-year-old sister, actress Jamie Lynn Spears, was good fodder for the media but it didn't cause her to lose a starring role in Zoey 101, a television show drawing a large viewership aged 9-14. When vice-presidential candidate Sarah Palin announced her 17-year-old daughter, Bristol, was five months pregnant, it gave teen pregnancy even more of a stamp of "normalcy."

What is it like to be a pregnant teen? Let teen mom Katie tell you about it. She is one of more than half a million teens facing unplanned pregnancies each year according to data from The National Campaign to Prevent Teen and Unplanned Pregnancy.

Available in bookstores and online through Amazon.com and other retailers.

Midnight Confessions:
True Stories of Adultery

Author: Pat Gaudette
Home & Leisure Publishing, Inc.
ISBN 978-0976121046
Available in Paperback, Kindle
& eBook Versions

Why does a person cheat? What type of person cheats? What type of person loves a cheat? Can adultery be forgiven? Can a marriage survive the adultery of one or both partners? Can a cheater be trusted not to cheat again?

Love and lust are powerful forces but with enough time and tears each of us comes to a point of decision making when faced with betrayal.

If you are the betrayed spouse, do you confront? Do you leave? Do you get revenge by cheating? If you are the betrayer, do you lie or tell the truth? Do you keep the affair going or end it to save your marriage? If you are the other person, do you accept what you can get or do you force confrontation to "get it all"?

Midnight Confessions: True Stories of Adultery *examines adultery from the adulterer's point of view, as well as that of the betrayed spouse and the other person. These are their stories in their words. Perhaps after reading their stories and the thought-provoking discussions in this book you will have a better understanding of the decision you need to make to fit your situation.*

Available in bookstores and online through Amazon.com and other retailers.

Advice for an Imperfect Single World
ISBN 978-0976121008

Advice for an Imperfect Married World
ISBN 978-0976121022

Available in Paperback, Kindle & eBook Versions

The outspoken "Queen of Hearts" is rarely without an opinion and since 1996 she has been sharing her thoughts about relationships in her advice column for the Friends and Lovers Web site. Advice for an Imperfect Married World focuses on situations facing married couples and couples involved in long term relationships. Advice for an Imperfect Single World, focuses on dating issues.

"Dear Queenie, me and my wife have split up and now we're trying to get back but she wants to be friends and take it slow. I'm afraid that we will just be friends and that's all. I want to know if we can be good friends and still be husband and wife and how can I show her that I want both?" - Peter.

"Peter, what you're really asking is how do you fast forward through all the friendship stuff and get right down to having sex again. While sex may be your top priority, developing a strong friendship is hers. If you are serious about wanting to repair your marriage you'll put your sex drive on hold and work on the friendship for now." - Queenie

Sparky the AIBO: Robot Dogs & Other Robotic Pets

Author: Pat Gaudette
Home & Leisure Publishing, Inc.
ISBN 978-09761210-7-7 Paperback
ISBN 978-09761210-6-0 Hardcover

On January 26, 2006, Sony Corporation announced they were discontinuing development and production of their AIBO Entertainment Robots. Sparky the AIBO takes a look at this wonderful consumer robot beginning with the ERS-110, released in 1999, through the exceptionally complex ERS-7M3, released October 2005.

AIBO models, software, accessories, forums, and web resources make this a must-have book for the AIBO enthusiast or the person interested in learning more about this delightful robot pet.

Amazon.com Customer Review: "Very nicely written and a cute book. It goes into each models of Aibo and their history. And, the writer's personal experiences with her Aibos. If you ever wonder why Aibo owners love their Aibo, read this book."

Available in bookstores and online through Amazon.com and other retailers.

Printed in Great Britain
by Amazon

48214399R00078